MONDAY'S PRAYER ON THE AIR

John Jackson

LAKELAND
MARSHALL, MORGAN & SCOTT
116 Baker Street
LONDON W1M 2BB

Copyright © John Jackson 1976

First published 1976

ISBN 0 551 00585 8

All rights reserved. No part of this publication may be reproduced, stored in a retrieval system, or transmitted in any form or by any means, electronic, mechanical, photocopying, recording or otherwise, without the prior permission of the copyright owner.

Printed in Great Britain by
Hunt Barnard Printing Ltd., Aylesbury, Bucks.

This book is dedicated with
love to my grandchildren
Richard and Sarah
Rachael and Nigel

CONTENTS

FOREWORD

By Sir Halford Reddish

I came to know John Jackson a long time ago through his 'Prayer for the Day' broadcasts on Monday mornings. He was certainly a character – a great character, one who inspired both respect and affection.

Although ill health had forced John to retire from his arduous work with the Whitechapel Mission, I know that I echo the feelings of many thousands of listeners when I say how glad we all were to be assured at that time that his Monday morning broadcasts were to continue: that he would still brighten the start of our working week with his inimitable few minutes of serious thought enlivened by an occasional characteristic flash of humour.

But alas! it was not to be. He died last November after a long period of ill health.

This third selection of his broadcast talks will be as popular as its predecessors, but for me and for thousands of others Monday will never be quite the same without that cheery north country voice with its 'Hello again, on another Monday morning'.

PREFACE

I worked with John Jackson as his BBC producer during his last two years. Every week I saw the flow of listeners' letters to him as they passed through my office: up to fifty in an ordinary week; six hundred in the ten days after he told us that illness had forced him to retire from the active Methodist ministry; nearly three hundred to his wife Florence and to the BBC in the two weeks after he died.

I have often thought about this response. I think I know why John became so dear to so many people who had never seen him. Of course he had one of those great north country voices that have enriched radio listening for fifty years. But it wasn't just that. It was the way he remembered everyone he had ever known, and called them up, and celebrated them and enjoyed them. Hearing him, you felt sure there was a place for you in this man's loving heart. And when at the end he commended you to the Master he served all his life with all his being, you felt God's blessing was yours.

I confess I did not think his words would stand up in print, divorced from that unforgettable voice.But that was before I understood his power. There is indeed loss, but the authentic John Jackson will be found in these pages.

PATRICK McENROE
BBC, London

THE BELIEFS OF BELIEF

Since I began broadcasting 'Prayer for the Day', the joy I have received from countless letters is something which has enriched my own life and faith immeasurably. Yet not a week has passed which did not contain one letter or more that was sad beyond words. These letters share with me personal tragedies, deep sorrows, acute shame and the like, and I must say a word or two about them.

The first and most important word to say is this – that words are the cheapest things in the world; and in so many, many ways it is easy to talk, but in some cases it is best to say nothing. Those of us upon whom kind Providence has always smiled do well to be careful when we presume to cross the threshold and blunder into the heartache of another man or his home.

I do feel, however, that I must go beyond that, and so the second word is a certain word that says quite emphatically that some sorrow and suffering can be explained, and the explanation is plain to every honest man. All of us have known instances where the sins of parents have caused children to suffer, and equally so, we have known cases where the sins of children have brought shame and sorrow to parents. All of us could quote examples from our experience of life that illustrates this only too plainly, and while we so often might wish it were otherwise, we know it is there – all too true.

My third word is one I want to shout – to say in capital letters, as it were. I can best do it by a true story. I recall a little boy of about five – a lovely, happy, curly-headed little boy – being knocked down and killed outright by a lorry. The little chap ran out into the street from the pathway up to his own home, chasing a ball. The driver of the lorry had no chance at all and in a flash it was all over. I heard a neighbour speak to the mother of that child soon after the accident and say, 'It's God's will and it must be borne.'

'No. No. No,' I said. 'If God were like that, I would have nothing to preach, no gospel – no good news – to offer. You see, I believe that all suffering is quite contrary to God's will everywhere.'

The fourth and last thing I want to say follows on from that, and it has meant so much to me with the passing of the years. We ministers see more than most folk of this kind of thing and we are often among the first to follow stark tragedy into the homes of our people. This is what I say – and I am being utterly honest: 'I do NOT know the reason why this has happened – it is quite beyond me. I just don't know WHY, but – I do know the God who does, and one day I know He will tell me and until then I must wait and trust and believe.'

Not now, but in the coming years –
It may be in the better land –
We'll read the meaning of our tears,
And there, some time we'll understand.

Yes, that's enough for me. And this I know too – the beliefs of belief are much easier to hold, come what may, than the beliefs of unbelief.

A prayer then to end:

Bless with Your loving presence all those who are in sorrow, suffering or shame. Help them by the power of Your good Spirit still to trust, even when they cannot trace, O Lord.

AMEN

'NEFF CAKE'

In most families there are things which belong to and are only understood by that family. In my family we have our private jokes and we only have to say one word; that word means nothing to anyone who may be with us at the time but it would be full of meaning to all my family. I know a family in the North who, when anyone dropped in on them unawares and stayed for a meal, would refer to the cake, or tarts, or pies as *Neff* cake, *Neff* tarts and *Neff* pies, and all the family knew not to take any because there was Not Enough For Family. I suppose it saved a lot of embarrassment. If I say to my wife – 'same as I said to our John Henry', or 'if you don't I will', or 'that's right Mr Jackson', or 'Tank-oo', they all refer to people and she would readily and easily identify them.

Some months ago, we were in the Midlands and talking to two of our grandest friends up there, and the conversation got round to family tiffs – or really, tiffs between man and wife. We all agreed that invariably they began with nothing yet sometimes they could grow into something quite large. Then our friends told us that as far back as their courting days they made a pact, that whenever things between them looked like getting out of hand and out of proportion, one of them would say, 'There aren't many boats on the canal tonight', and that would end it. I don't know why they chose that phrase, but they did, and it has always worked. I think that's grand, it must have saved them from many unnecessary heartaches. I know that it meant one thing that is very important – they never let the sun go down on their wrath; or, to put it more plainly, they never went to bed not speaking, having fallen out.

I suppose we are all concerned about the nations who are divided internally, and also with their neighbours. It always leads to sorrow and tragedy, with the very old and the very young as the chief sufferers. I suppose we go on to say, 'Yes, very sad, but there is nothing we can do about it.' Too far away, too many people, too much of everything involved – and there simply isn't anything we can do about it.

Be that as it may, I do know, being a minister, that all too often there are divisions, sometimes very serious divisions, in our individual relationships. The spirit of forgiveness is absent and any thought of coming together is thought to be a sign of weakness. Those very things could be spoiling your home, your church, your family, your school, shop, factory floor, and managerial suite this very day.

Never mind who is right or who is wrong – this is the day to say, 'There aren't many boats on the canal tonight.' To come together in sweet reasonableness, to begin to forgive and forget. An old hymn I know has the line, 'O be ye reconciled'. It means you and God – you and Jesus. I think it's vital advice, but if you are reconciled with Jesus then it must follow as the night the day, that you will do all in your power to be reconciled with all men.

Anyway, let me end by making a plea that you and your loved ones have some phrase – you pick your own and decide today to use it as my friends do about canal boats – so that no quarrel, no argument, no difference even, begins to spoil and mar and separate.

Our prayer asks:

Reconcile me with Yourself, Lord Jesus, and fill me with the spirit of reconciliation towards all others. For Your name's sake.

AMEN

DO YOU LIVE WHERE YOU ARE?

For the first thirty years of my life I had only heard about miners, or read about them. It was no wonder, then, that based on such weak and unreliable evidence I had a completely wrong impression of them. I thought, when I bothered to think at all, that their lives were made up, by and large, of pit, pub and pigeons. How quickly this misconception altered over the next twenty years, when for much of that time I lived in mining areas, and got to know and to respect so very many of them. I also went down a coal mine – my goodness that altered my views! I resolved that day that if anyone was relying on me to bring them some coal up, then it was a certain fact they would have to burn wood. I can't, for the life of me, understand why anybody goes down the pit to work – not at any price.

But, I want to go on now to tell of one particular miner who became a great friend of mine. His life was not circumscribed and hedged in. He didn't believe the world began and ended with coal. He could talk to you about tickling trout and would share with you the secrets of the countryside. He could direct you to some of the lesser known but loveliest parts of Shropshire and North Wales. It was through him that I was introduced to 'Fingal's Cave' and heard the 'Messiah' with Sir Malcolm Sargent and full orchestra. He read good books and did a scale drawing in Indian ink of the gates at Chirk Castle. I saw him make a pair of gates, in oak, big enough to take a motor-car, and those gates will still be there long after he and I are gone – a splendid job he made of them. It was a great sight too, to watch him clean and tend his motor-bike. I don't see him very often now, but he's retired and the last time I saw him, do you know what he'd done? He had taken a block of hard wood, I should think about twelve to fourteen inches long and maybe three inches square, and he had painstakingly worked on this for hours and hours and he showed me the end product. It was three links in a wooden chain; each link moved freely within its neighbour, yet the whole had been carved out of one piece of wood and there were no joins. I keep telling myself I must have a go at that.

I'm hoping that you are filling your life. Kipling wrote about 'filling every minute with sixty seconds worth of distance run.' So many folk today are unutterably bored, and boredom often leads to other problems, I know. One of the grandest promises of Jesus was that He came not only so that we might have life, but that we might have it more abundantly. He made that offer to you and me.

When I retire, obviously I am going to live somewhere else, and someone wrote to me and reminded me: 'It doesn't matter where you live, what does matter is that you live where you are.' My miner friend Geoff would say 'Amen' to that, and so would I.

Our prayer this morning asks:

Prevent us, O Lord, from being idle and bored. Show us grand horizons and fulfil in us your promise of abundant living. For Your name's sake.

AMEN

THE MIDDLE MILES

I don't know what brought it up, but the discussion was all about the marathon walking race. I really don't know why I got involved at all, since my long distance walk these days is round the block, and that's only weather permitting.

The point at issue was, which was the hardest part? Somebody said it was the start – setting off, knowing that you had all those long gruelling miles ahead of you. Maybe so, but at least at the beginning you are fresh and you've trained for this very feat and may well be raring to go. The end, somebody else said – that's the toughest part. You have padded away for mile upon mile upon mile and gradually your zeal and energy have been sapped away and now you ache all over and every breath is painful – at every step now you are beginning to wonder if it won't be the last. Here it was pointed out that when you reach this stage you are near to or in the arena, and the crowds are rising and cheering and all this puts new life into you – you are carried along by their support and enthusiasm over that dreadful last half mile or so.

Well, there's a lot of truth in all that, but for me I think the toughest part is the middle part. No crowds cheering here, and no fresh impetus. Now it's just a matter of steadily keeping on keeping on – the humdrum miles – nothing spectacular or exciting, just sheer plod and stickability are the thing in the middle miles.

Isn't it something like that in trying to follow Jesus? When you decide to do so, the initial thrill may well bear you forward as though you were being carried – propelled – and away you go, sprinting off down the straight, and you too have cheers and encouragement. It happened to me, so I know. Also I have met over the years lots and lots of folk who were nearing the end of the race, and they had about them a glow of contentment, a joy of a purpose achieved – they have kept the faith, nearly finished the course and the crown is in sight as promised.

Ah, yes, but probably most of us are in the middle years – the middle miles – and probably too we're finding it tough going. Well, it should be like that. Following Jesus isn't a hundred-yard sprint – just the odd flashy burst; it's something which belongs to all day and every day. The Christian life has no place for part-timers – for the fitful and the showy. Many of you will be able to recall Roger Bannister's face on that great day when he became the first man to run the mile in under four minutes – it was covered with sweat and agony. Have we ever looked like that in our travel in the steps of our Master? I once read about a chap who told another chap that he had decided some weeks previously to become a Christian, and the chap said, 'Good – how much does it hurt?'

Oh! I know all about the joy of following Christ, but I'm sure now that it only comes to those who stick it out, fair weather and foul, sunshine and shadow – start, finish and above all, middle.

Our prayer this morning asks:

Help us in our following You, Lord Jesus, and especially when we feel we are going it alone and the way is tedious, lonesome and long. For Your name's sake.

AMEN

A PRESENT FOR MUM

The main 'outreach' to use the modern in-word, or the main mission of the Whitechapel Mission where I work, has always been towards men and boys. Its founder, the Rev. Thomas Jackson (no relation of mine by the way), saw this as his work, and from then right up to today this emphasis has been maintained.

I'm sure, too, that over all those years just as now there will have been times when my four predecessors have asked themselves, 'What good are we doing? What's it all about? Is it worth while carrying on?' And then, also like me, they have been given to see that one only does what God calls you to do and then, having done it, to the best of your ability, you leave it to Him. Often I have had to remind myself that when I am at the end of my tether, God is never at the end of His. Also, it is important to add that all along the road, from time to time, a light shines and you are allowed to see a glimpse of the harvest, an evidence that all is far from being in vain.

Yes, it must have always been like that, because recently I had a letter from a lady in Kent, and I'm going to quote you part of it now. It all happened more than twenty years ago. She wrote: 'I was working in London and David (a boy from the Whitechapel Mission Working Lads' Hostel) was brought to the firm for whom I worked and engaged as an office boy.

'He was the eldest of four children, his father was a semi-invalid and his mother had to work to support the family; the only holiday he had known was going to the hop-fields. Then came the highlight of his life – he was to go to the Scout camp in the summer. The day before his holiday commenced I gave him half-a-crown (twelve-and-a-half new pence). His eyes lit up and he said, "Thank you Mrs Wilson – now I can buy my Mum a present".'

She goes on to say, 'That boy must be at least thirty-five

years old now but I have never forgotten him, nor how humble he made me feel that day.'

Aye, and so say all of us – for what was true of David isn't always true of us. The last thought in his head was himself and the first thought was someone else – his Mum.

All I'm trying to say is so simple that it sounds trite to say it, but I'm going to, and it's this. There would be no more problems in homes and families, in industry and civic affairs, nor indeed among the nations of the world, if everyone lived and acted as David did. Far too many of us are turning out those words like 'I' and 'me' and 'mine' – and those other words – 'his', 'ours', 'theirs', pass our lips all too rarely. Whatever we might have, has only been entrusted to us for our lifetime, and I'm very sure there is a day of accountability, and on that day we shall be separated – on one side there will be those who, receiving half-a-crown, use it wholly for themselves, and on the other side there will be those like David who spend it on someone else – for love's sake. For me that is quite plainly the teaching of Jesus.

Well, there will be other boys and men – scores of them about whom I shall never hear – that were influenced at Whitechapel, and they too will have taken something of Jesus with them, after meeting Him there – this I know is still happening.

My prayer this morning asks:

Help all of us, O Lord, having received also to give, having got also to share, and above all, having heard of your love, to tell others. For Your name's sake.

AMEN

WHARTON BRIDGE

Some of you will know where I am talking about when I mention Wharton Bridge. When I was living at home in Cheshire it was the second bridge, after the second station, north of Crewe on the main line – Crewe to Scotland or Liverpool. It was more than that – it was the point to turn back for home on every pleasant Sunday afternoon as a group of us took a walk after Sunday School. It was the road bridge on which I could stand as a boy and see my father's signal cabin and I've stood there many times and waved and waved until he waved back.

It was a favourite place for us lads (and girls too – if I remember aright) to stand, as the old steam engines roared underneath, going at sixty to seventy miles per hour, having got full steam up after the Crewe stop or else making the last lap before slowing down to enter Crewe on the southbound journey. There was something fascinating in being completely engulfed in the smoke for a few seconds – you could smell the power and feel the magic of the iron road in some strange, mysterious way.

Going under the bridge northward, the trains would then pass my Dad in his signal box and it was his job to make sure not only that the train passed, but that *all* of it passed. His rules compelled him to ensure that every train had a tail light on the last coach and by seeing this – daylight or dark – he then knew that the complete train had gone by and not, as indeed could and did happen very occasionally, a part of it, leaving some carriage, carriages or wagon still blocking the line, maybe somewhere out of sight. Nothing less than all was enough.

For many years now I have been meeting people with worries, fears, guilt and the like, and they have quite often tried many remedies for their ills. Quite often, too, they have got partial relief. Some of the stress has gone, the symptoms are not quite so acute, they think they are perhaps better able to cope with life. Some have tried everything – drink, drugs, analysis, hypnosis, group therapy, electric shock and the rest – and yet all is not well, all is not cured. Maybe there only lurks a nagging doubt, but there it is in the pit of the stomach, eating away at true peace, until you have got to label it an ulcer and then the treatment is drastic.

Nothing less than *all* will do. In those cases where the trouble truly has its roots in sin and guilt, there is only one cure that is a full and complete remedy, and that is the forgiveness and renewal that Jesus promises to anyone who is truly sorry and turns to Him in true repentance. He, and He alone, is able to wipe out the past and make us – or better still, remake us – into a new person. With Jesus it is never a matter of partial healing, of glossing or veneering over, of patching up for the time being – He makes ANEW.

We chapel folk sing sometimes about being, 'ransomed, healed, restored, forgiven,' and if that isn't something to sing about, I don't know what is. That way, a man's ills vanish as the train smoke always did on Wharton Bridge.

A prayer to end:

Lord Jesus Christ, forgive us wherein we need forgiveness,
Remake us and rid us of all our ills.
Go with us, then, and fulfil our joy. For Your name's sake.
AMEN

DIRECTIONAL AERIAL

Staying in a lovely West Midlands village on convalescence at the home of my son-in-law and daughter, I found my little grand-daughter both a tonic and an alarm clock.

One of the fascinations of staying there is that my son-in-law is a radio ham enthusiast – one of those chaps who speak to Hobart, Hong Kong and Bombay from their own back room. (Or should that be Halifax, Huddersfield and Bradford? I'm not sure.) Recently, he has added another item to all the amazing gadgets and whatnots – he's got a directional aerial. This aerial is on the roof of the house and yet, sitting at his radio receiver and transmitter, he is able to cause his aerial to rotate and point to any point on the compass that he wishes. I gather this can give greatly improved results and makes a considerable difference to the whole undertaking. It's quite fun to stand in the back garden and to watch this aerial go round and back until it is pointing in the best direction for what is required at any given time. All of which gave me to think.

The old Jews used to think that for them to get in touch with God it helped if, when they spoke to Him in prayer, they turned towards Jerusalem. When they were beaten in battle and taken captive to other countries they still, at prayer time, turned towards Jerusalem. It happened to a chap called Daniel, and he not only turned towards Jerusalem, but in the place where he was imprisoned he had a window made to open towards Jerusalem. He was determined to leave nothing to chance in keeping in touch with headquarters.

I'm not thinking so much now about praying, but rather about preparation for prayer. Getting lined up, focused and prepared before the actual prayer itself is ever offered up. Especially I am thinking of the preparation which Jesus said we needed to make before we made our requests known.

He said that reconciliation – the making up of broken

relationships, the forgiving of others – has to be attended to before we say our prayers.

Over the years as a minister I've known nothing more sad than broken homes and families – staying broken because no one would forgive, and even staying broken so long that the parties involved have almost forgotten what it was all about in the first place.

Perhaps this is the day for you to prepare for your prayers to reach their destination by preparing the way in an act of forgiveness.

Perhaps not having done so is the reason why you are beginning to wonder why there seems to be little or no real response to your prayers of late.

If you went to that other person in forgiveness and said, 'There's nothing between us now', then when next you said your prayers God would say the same to you.

What a difference it would make.

A prayer – there's only one will do:

Forgive us our trespasses as we also have forgiven others their trespasses against us.

AMEN

LILY CLARK

I don't think we have ever met since we left school – or maybe we have once, I'm just not sure. We were in the same form and I have good cause to remember her because she was nearly always, week in, week out, in each subsequent class, top of the form. Others tried, and tried hard, but rarely – and I mean rarely – did anyone overtake Lily.

I was thrilled to bits recently when she wrote to me and recalled those days at school together, but it wasn't what she wrote about school itself that I want to tell you. No, it was something else, and I'll quote from her letter.

Speaking of going to school, she wrote, 'Rigged up in my clogs, I walked over the locks (on the river Weaver), up several muddy fields to the Irishman's shanty at the farm above the valley, changed into my school shoes, got my bicycle from there and cycled to the railway station. Then on the "Dodger" to Over and Wharton station, a mile walk up to the school, same journey in reverse each evening (ravenously hungry, lock keepers' wages didn't run to bought hot school dinners).' And then she adds, 'How times have changed!'

How right she is. And don't think for one single moment that I want us ever to go back to many of the dark and evil things that belong to those days – I don't. But I do know that Lily was proud to go to that school, and she knew and accepted the fact that along with that privilege, she had her responsibilities. She was awarded a scholarship and in return she gave her best, not only in her school work but also in the sheer daily endeavour of getting to and from the school.

I had the great privilege of going to a proper Methodist training college under a staff of truly great men. During my years there I never lost the sense of wonder; indeed I still have it – wonder that I should ever have had the chance to go there at all. To live in that old building in its splendid grounds, where over many years great men had taught and trained. Richmond gave me so much, and I like to think that then and now I have been able to offer something in return. In those days, student participation meant that they taught and I tried to learn first of all.

We've not had much snow where I live this year, but watching the odd snow showers I recalled one day watching some children sledging, and thought, 'My – I'd like a go!' But as I watched on, it dawned on me that when you rode down, with all its thrills – then you had to drag the sledge right to up the top of the hill again.

My biggest joy is to have Jesus as my Saviour and Lord – I accept Him so gladly. It would be quite mean and meaningless if I ever forgot for one single moment that when Jesus said 'Come', and I came to Him, He then said, 'Go and be my disciple.'

Yes, as Lily reminded me, there's a cross that saves and a cross to carry.

A prayer to end:

If we take and never give, if we have and only hold, if we ride and never push, if we bask and never reflect, if we are loved and never loving, forgive us, Lord.

AMEN

PLASTIC POSIES

Even though it all happened maybe ten years ago now, I can still see it all quite plainly, and I can even now feel the astonishment that came over me when I realised what was happening. My wife and I were having an early holiday on the south coast of Cornwall. The weather was what my mother would have described as fair to middling. On the day in question it was one of those days when it was too nice to stay in the hotel and yet not inviting enough to go far afield. We decided we would wrap up a bit and sit in one of the sheltered alcoves at the front of the hotel. There was a lovely outlook right out to sea, and we were quite happy quietly reading and looking and, I guess, dozing the time away.

We had not been there long when a flashy sports car zoomed up the drive and out got a young fellow. He had with him a couple of large cases and these he unpacked. It soon became obvious he was a photographer. For half an hour or so he appeared to me to prance hither and thither and look at the hotel through his fingers and through the camera from every vantage point on the whole frontage, and yet he never took one single photograph.

A large grey van then drew up and two men got out and opened the back doors and began to unload it. They got out scores upon scores of artificial flowers and plants. They then began to plant them – this is where the amazement came in. They filled the borders in which there was not a flower, they filled pots and tubs and ledges and window boxes, they covered wall copings and the porch until everywhere looked like a cross between Chelsea and Shrewsbury on Show Day. When all this false splendour was in place, the photographer began. He really went to town, and I can only suppose that before long, colourful and floral brochures of the said hotel would be flooded out to the nation, and no doubt obtain the hoped-for response. Well, well – things are not always what they seem.

When I was a boy, you had a best suit – for Sundays only. My father once said to me about a chap in the church, 'Pity – he could have been great, but now he puts his best suit away and his Christianity with it.' It was sham and show, like those artificial flowers in Cornwall.

There's nothing new about this. It was very true in the time of Jesus, and has been ever since. In a way I'm sure it's true of all of us. We all do our share of shop-window dressing – making things look better for the others to see, having to resort to the artificial because the real just isn't there.

Our forgiving Lord wants us, I know, to go on trying, to rely more upon Him – to know and believe that it is possible for us to be real and true in His service. The best thing we can do is to ask Him to help us – there is no other way.

Lord Jesus Christ, may you so help us as our Saviour and so rule in our lives as Lord, that every part is filled with Thee and all our being truly speaks at all times of Thee and of Thy love. For Thy name's sake.

AMEN

CHIMNEY POTS

I counted them several times. There's really not much to do in hospital during those days when you are on the way to recovery. You are not really up to reading anything of any depth, and there are all sorts of interruptions. It's their routine you follow and not the devices and desires of your own heart.

The first time I went into hospital at the age of eight, it was a little hospital, which stood in fields with long rolling views across the pastures and meadows. There were cattle and flowers and trees to see. Anything more remote from Tower Hamlets, London, it would be hard to imagine. So, as I say, I counted them several times, and within the view from my ward window there were ninety-three. They had been there, most of them, for very many years. Some of them were very ornate. A few stood in splendid isolation, others were in sixes, or even twelve in once case. On every roof within view there were chimneys and on these, as I say, there were ninety-three chimney pots.

I used to picture the days gone by when from every one of them, for most of the year, smoke would issue from the fires burning below in the grates. There was warmth and the warmth was important to life for many. Now, of course, even if there is a grate still, there's no fire, there's no smoke and the chimney pots – all ninety-three of them – are useless, meaningless, not what they seem; and if you took them all away nobody would be any worse off. They are only a bit of outward sham and show, of things that once were.

There were a lot of folk in the time of Jesus like those chimney pots. To all intents and purposes they looked to be God's men. They were found in the right places, they said the right things and did the right things, indeed, some of them were ornate and dressed up for the part as it were. Inside, which is always where Jesus looks, there was no fire, no warmth, no compassion or comfort. They too, like the

London chimneys, might just as well not have been there.

A sad enough story, but it's even sadder to know that it's just as true today; and what's more, it's often true of our lives – the shape, the form, the fashion, of the men of Jesus but nothing more. The fire has gone out, and the ashes are all that remain.

When I was on the railway, in certain places there were signals that didn't work; they stayed fixed in one position and were called dummies. What a pity if somebody, instead of counting chimney pots, is counting Christians, and they have to pass us over as dummies. I'm speaking now especially to those of you in whose lives the fire has gone out, those of you who 'did run well,' those of you who weren't always lukewarm, those of you who ask yourselves, 'Where is the blessedness I knew when first I saw the Lord?'

There never will again be any smoke coming out of my ninety-three chimney pots, but that needn't be true of us. If the fire has gone out and the glow has passed away, the Master is willing and waiting to rekindle the sacred flame, to burn with intensity in our hearts, to enable us to shed abroad the warmth of His forgiveness in love.

Now let's end with a prayer –

Forgive us, O Lord, if we have grown cold in Thy service, fallen out of the race, been diverted or side-tracked. Rekindle within our hearts a burning desire to think and speak and live for Thee. Through Jesus Christ our Lord.

AMEN

THE LONDON HOSPITAL

During the three weeks I was in hospital I had far more time than I usually have to think, and I suppose automatically I thought about hospitals. I've known them over many years now as a visitor and chaplain, but it's quite different knowing them as a patient.

We all know a hospital is a place of skill, and in many cases of teaching. It is a place of pain; indeed, I read recently of a great hospital and it was described as a city of pain. It is a place of experiment and research, of well-nigh miracle surgery. Yes, it's all of those added together, I suppose, but that doesn't cover what a hospital is to me.

A man named Baron von Hugel once wrote in a letter to his niece, 'Nothing matters like caring.' Yes, for me that's getting nearer the truth – a hospital is a place of caring. But more than that, because it is a place of caring, for me it is a part of the Kingdom of God here on earth. You remember, when Jesus was separating those in the Kingdom and those outside, he said to those who were in, 'You cared,' and to those left outside, 'You didn't care.'

Why should it be that six, eight or so girls should have bothered themselves about me, a stranger to them? Yes, bothered about me, night and day, and especially when I was too ill to bother about myself. They did not ask who I was, or what I was, or what I'd got. My country of birth, my colour of skin, my bank balance, my connections were not gone into. They simply cared for me, all of them, as best they knew how.

It is lovely sometimes to see what are called miniatures, small reproductions of larger and greater things. My wife has a ring and a brooch, both of which have miniature reproductions of the 'Laughing Cavalier' – they are very lovely to look at, even though they are so much smaller than the real thing.

I'm one of those people who believe that one day, right

will utterly prevail, that the kingdoms of this world will become the kingdoms of our God and of His Christ. Yes, in spite of the seeming sadness, madness and badness of this sin-sick world, I most surely believe these things. The first Easter Day was victory day, and we Christians are living on the winning side of Easter. Easter renews my faith in a living and loving Lord. Jesus the Conqueror reigns. But on top of that, my faith is renewed and strengthened because for a while I saw His Kingdom in miniature and dwelt within it.

Far round our world this day there are, I'm sure, countless miniatures, not only in hospital but in every city, town and village, north, south, east and west – places where nothing matters like caring; places where you can catch a glimpse of the Kingdom of God.

A prayer then to end:

O God, our Loving Father, daily we pray, Thy Kingdom come on earth as it is in Heaven. We thank Thee for those places where it has already come, and ask Thee to bless and prosper all their labours, until Thy Kingdom of love and caring has fully come. For Christ's sake.

AMEN

ST PATRICK'S DAY

A special hello on St Patrick's Day to all my many friends in Ireland, and especially to the scores of people who have been kind enough to write to me over the years about my broadcasts on Monday mornings. I have so much valued your loving interest and promised prayers.

I have been fortunate on two occasions to visit Ireland. The first visit was to Dublin and the second to Belfast. So often I have wished to see more and more of that green island. When I worked on the railway at Crewe, there was a man working in the telegraph office with a lovely voice – I have only to close my eyes and I can hear him singing now 'The Mountains of Mourne'.

With that little background I would be a fool to take sides, to pass judgments or to be dogmatic about the situation over recent years. I'm not a fool, however, when I tell you my heart yearns for all of you there that you should have helpful days and peaceful nights and that wounds might be healed and many prayers answered.

Assuring you then of a continued place in our prayers I'm going to presume to tell you a story. There are only two characters in this story and what more fitting names could they have than Pat and Mick? For as long as anybody thereabouts could remember they had been neighbours, and for a couple of decades they had both been widowers and lived alone. In everything they differed except in their hatred of each other and in their age. They were poles apart in religion and politics, in their sporting allegiances, in their leisure pastimes, hours of going to bed, and hours of getting up. Not a day passed but they had one good slanging match over the garden wall, and if you'd had to print what was said on these occasions, the ink would need to be deep red and blue!

So they lived and so they hated, and the years rolled by. Their behaviour towards each other was a legend in the neighbourhood, a cause of mild amusement and yet of an inner deep disgust.

One winter's night, returning home from their separate activities, there was a black frost and fog. Crossing the road almost together they were knocked down by a hit-and-run motorist. Eventually they came to in hospital and were sent home – Pat was now blinded and would never see again, Mick was crippled from the waist down and would never walk again and was confined to a wheelchair.

About a fortnight after getting home, on a glorious spring morning, Mick heard a gentle tap on his back door and struggled with his wheelchair until he was able to open the door. There, standing at the door, was his enemy of the years, Patrick – blind Patrick now – from next door. In a very quiet voice he said, 'Mick, I can't go beyond the confines of my own home because I can't see where I am going, neither can you for you are unable to walk. It struck me that if you sat in your chair and steered and I pushed it from the rear, you and I could get together and go almost anywhere and do anything'.

So a new legend has sprung up, not now of hatred and intolerance but of love and partnership and sharing.

A prayer to end:

Look down, O Lord, this day, especially upon all Thy people in the whole of Ireland. By the operation of Thy good Spirit draw them all so near to Thee that they are inevitably nearer to each other. Thwart all the devices of evil men and prosper all endeavours to bring about unity, concord and peace.

Forgive all of us for our corporate share in the sins that inevitably bring sadness. Through Jesus Christ our Lord.

AMEN

FLOWERS NOW, PLEASE

For almost twenty years as boy and man I lived in a house which was so situated that the majority of folk in that mid-Cheshire town wishing to go to the local churchyard had to pass my home. It became rather fascinating with the passing of the years to notice the regulars. These were the folk who, week in, week out, spring, summer, autumn and winter, went along to the churchyard to tidy up the grave, cut the surrounding grass and to renew the dead flowers with fresh ones.

I'm sure that in very many cases what they did was a good and laudable thing, but was it always like that? In a small town that size we all tended to know, or to think we knew, everything about everybody else. Well, perhaps it wasn't always true we knew everything, but my goodness I've looked through our front window many times and thought, 'Why didn't he give her flowers when she was living? Why didn't he find the time he now spends visiting her grave, to spend with her while she was still living?' One poor woman I remember was pushed around in a bath chair everywhere she went for quite a few years. Then he died, the one-man power motor that moved her bath chair, and bless me, then she used to walk past regularly to put flowers on his grave.

When you went into the actual churchyard itself sometimes, and read the names on the gravestones, we locals knew practically every one of them, and I've looked at some of the biggest, the most expensive, the most ostentatious, and wondered why. Sometimes it used to seem to me that the big gravestone at the end was covering up a thousand small omissions of thoughtfulness and love over a lifetime.

Let me say again, and let me underline it, there were many glorious exceptions to the generalisations I've just been making. I was, however, I'm sure, sufficiently near to the truth for me to plead for flowers now rather than later.

A few weeks ago I should have been speaking one evening in a Surrey village and was unable to go at the last minute due to illness. A dear friend of mine went instead, and I'm sure they had a great time. A few days later I received one of the loveliest bunches of flowers I've ever seen. Those dear folk in that little village wanted me to know they had missed my going and wanted to wish me a full and speedy recovery to health and strength again. Well, I'm perfectly sure that those flowers brought more joy and comfort to my wife and myself than six dozen orchids will do if somebody puts them on the gravestone after I've gone.

Once upon a time, ten fellows were suffering from a dreadful illness called leprosy. Jesus cured them, made them whole and well again, and one of them, only one mind you, bothered to stop and say thank you. I don't know, perhaps the others popped along with a few flowers later on when they heard He was dead and buried and laid in the tomb of Joseph of Arimithea. I don't know, I say, but I do know it was far better to give to Him that simple bouquet of gratitude and to say thank you at the time.

What I've tried to say to you applies to the whole of life, but nowhere is it more important than in our homes. Make your mind up this moment that as for you and yours, you are going to give the flowers now.

A prayer to end then:

Give us the grace, O God, that knows how to accept kindness and how to show it every day and in every part of our lives, especially within that blessed place called home. Through Jesus Christ our Lord.

AMEN

CHAPEL TEAS

It came as a great surprise to me at the time – I couldn't think why on earth they did it, but they did, and as far as I know they still do. They arrange for you to have a medical examination when you offer as a candidate for the Methodist ministry.

It's all so long ago now, I can't really recall what happened in any detail, but with the passing of the years I have grown to suspect more and more that the test was an attempt to ensure that you had hollow legs and blotting paper innards. You see, as those years have rolled by and I reflect on the amount of tea I have drunk, for the Kingdom's sake as it were, I am convinced now that only someone with those attributes could possibly have consumed so much liquid. There aren't many occasions among the events that take place at the chapel when room and place is not found for the inevitable cup of tea; and of course, on top of the chapel gallons there are the visitation gallons and the manse gallons.

In my first appointment as a minister I recall attending one of those chapel teas on the banks of the Humber. There was nothing special about the tea – it was typical of all those I had had before and have had since. There is, however, a good reason for me to remember that tea-drinking occasion. Indeed, I would be sorry ever to forget it, it taught me so much.

Sitting almost opposite to me was a very lovely girl; but she was not just lovely in a physical sense, but also in her manner. She brought to that table at which I sat, laughter and gaiety and a spirit of thankfulness that seemed to spread amongst the whole group of us sitting near by. She was sitting at the table when I got to it and after the meal was over and folk began to get up and leave, she sat on. I stayed on too, chatting to her, for I had nowhere to go until I spoke in an hour or so's time at the evening meeting. For quite a little while there were just the two of us chatting on until eventually, as she had said he would, her husband arrived. He gave her a kiss and drew her chair back from the table and it wasn't until then that I knew that both her legs were in irons and she was only able to move because he picked her up and carried her to her wheelchair parked in the outside porch.

I wondered then, and I've wondered many times since, what sort of person I would be to have tea with if I suffered and was handicapped like she was. Would folk sit with me for an hour or so and never hear me moan and groan, even though I would have plenty of cause for doing both? I rather doubt it. I'm inclined to get quite cross if I only knock my thumb up or have a bit of backache.

That day, too, has reminded me of something else I've tried never to forget. If I had got up from the tea table along with the majority, as I might easily have done, I should never even have known what she had to endure all day and every day. I've tried to remember this, you see, because there are so many occasions in life for all of us when we just have no idea at all of the load – aye, of the cross – that many smiling and uncomplaining people carry through every moment of every day.

I did learn, by the way, something of their secret. This girl and her husband knew and loved Jesus, and they found help from Him – help enough to come smiling through.

A prayer to end then:

Lord Jesus, bless all those folk who have heavy burdens to bear. Share the strain with them. Prevent me from ever making harsh judgments on other people by reminding me that I do not know the full story. For Your name's sake.

AMEN

SOUNDS I MISS

Some time in the dark days of November I paid a visit to an ancient West Country city to attend a book fayre. For me it was a very enjoyable occasion, except that when it came time to come back again to London, I didn't seem to allow myself sufficient time. You see, anybody who huffs and puffs like I do needs a long time to travel a little way.

Well, I got to the station and there, standing at the platform of my departure, was an express train. I rushed as best as I'm able up the stairs of the footbridge, across the bridge, down the stairs and literally flopped into the carriage of the train standing at the platform. I eased my overcoat off and tried to relax and recover my breath, when suddenly a voice from the public address system announced, 'The train standing at such a platform (I've forgotten now), is due to depart for Birmingham.' I was in the wrong train! I grabbed my overcoat and tumbled out of the train, just as the guard's whistle blew and it started away.

I collapsed on to a Post Office truck and lay there in the gloom and damp. I can recall feeling very cross at the time – you see, I resented the fact, for the few minutes in which I was sure I was going to die, that I wouldn't die with the dignity of being within sight and sound of a real railway engine, a steam engine. I resented closing this earthly life under the shadow of an electrical box with antlers ons.

Well, as is obvious, I did recover on that Post Office truck, I did catch the next train which was the right one, I did get back to London and home and indeed, here I am many months later able to tell the tale.

Thinking of there being no sound of steam engines on that big railway station, I wonder what kind of sounds you miss in these days? Every morning in the early years of my life. I would hear the clip-clop of men and women wearing clogs going to work, and later on, the same sound of boys and girls going to school. Many times during every day I heard the sound of horses' hooves on hard roads, the cry of the rag-and-bone man, the selling of wares by the man on his stall at the Saturday night market beneath the light and odour of the naptha flickering flares. Living where I do now, I must rely on memory for the singing of birds and the rustle of the trees and the babbling brook.

But there is something else that I do not hear away from my home these days. Only on rare occasions does anyone today seem to bother to say 'Grace', to say thank you before their meals. Funny, isn't it, in these days when we know that half the world is underfed and hundreds upon hundreds have nothing and die – funny, isn't it, that we can't even bother to say, 'Thank you'.

Two business men dining in a London hotel noticed the man who came to their table for his evening meal, put his hands together and close his eyes. They asked him what he was doing. 'Well,' he said, 'I'm simply saying thank you for the good food I am going to eat.' They looked at each other and him for a little while in amazement, and then one of them said to him, 'You know, we don't bother to do that kind of thing here in the City.' The farmer pondered on this for a minute, then he replied, 'Come to think of it, my pigs back in Yorkshire yonder, don't either.'

Now a prayer to end:

Thank You, God, for everything.

AMEN

FLATMEN

My grandfather on my mother's side, was a ship's captain. I sometimes went as a boy to see the ships in port and I can recall some of their names even today – *Herald of Peace – Decempedes – Nil Desperandum – Phoenix – Vale Royal – Firefly*. They were the fleet of the Salt Company on the River Weaver and they plied between Winsford and Runcorn and Liverpool, along the Weaver and the Mersey. Small craft and a small crew maybe, but these flatmen, as they were sometimes called because of their nearly flat-bottomed boats, were proud, and justly proud, of their craft and there was due promotion to the Commodore of the line.

Happy, busy days sometimes – sad, hard days of no work or short time at others, but it was a joy to see the river, even from the town bridge, when things were really active and work was plentiful. They were men who went down to the sea in ships even if those ships were only salt packets.

There used to be a story told of how one of them was moored along the quay side somewhere in the Mersey, and I guess it could well have been the least of all the ships about, and perhaps it wasn't very sparkling and newly painted. Anyway, the story goes that someone passing along the shore looked down at her and began to scoff and laugh and then said to the young lad, the hand in his teens, 'This isn't one of the Cunard Line is it?' 'No,' he replied, 'it's perhaps not much of a ship at all, but we have got the finest captain on the river.'

He was quite satisfied to have sailed under a good captain. In this island home of ours, for many centuries there must have been scores of men who made that claim with a deal of pride. They had sailed under Drake, Nelson, Beattie and the like – great captains.

In my lifetime I've listened to some severe criticism of the Church and I could add to it at times even about my own Church. I've also heard some severe and yet often justified criticisms of my fellow Christians – the crew of H.M.S. *Church* as it were – and I suppose you could most fittingly use the nautical word motley, to describe us, for all too often we must seem to be a poor mixed bag and we must often leave a great deal to be desired.

All right – but say what you will about the craft and crew, nevertheless we do sail under the greatest, grandest and best captain that ever was.

In the end, it seems to me, nothing matters except following Jesus. Letting Him transform my life until my words and deeds and thoughts are like His. I keep on trying to do that, and though I often fail, I know that in the end all will be well. I know we shall arrive in port safe home with Christ at the helm.

Are you sailing under the finest Captain? There's always a place for you in His crew.

My prayer:

Jesus, Saviour, pilot me.

AMEN

'GONE HOME WITH A FRIEND'

Like me, you will have seen those competitions where you are asked to complete the verse, the couplet, the epitaph; and the one that is adjudged the best wins the prize. I want you to do just that, but I'm sorry to have to tell you I am not offering any prizes! Maybe you can cheat, because you could well know the original as well as I do, but here it is anyway. It's the first line of a hymn with the last word missing – 'Rejoice for a brother — '.

Now, how are you going to complete that so that you feel you really can rejoice about this brother of yours? What is it you would want to happen to him – or, if you like, to yourself – so that you could and would truly rejoice and be glad? I can think of lots of endings that lots of people would want to add, and they would earnestly believe that in so doing, they would be putting their finger at the heart and source of true happiness. Things like – Rejoice for a brother – who's rich – who's fit – who's won the pools – got two houses – two cars – – a star – an idol – famous – beautiful – young – in power – – ruling – pleasing himself – and you, too, could add your own ending.

Well, the original ending was – 'Rejoice for a brother DECEASED'. Yes, a brother who's dead – for it's the first line of a funeral hymn. The second line goes on to say, 'Our loss is his infinite gain.'

Is that how you look at death? And I don't mean death in the abstract – death in the newspaper obituaries – death round the corner – third house up, blue curtains, Mrs . . . you are not sure who. But death in your own home – someone near and dear to you. Can you rejoice then? Well, I think it all depends on what you think about death. I can rejoice in spite of my deep sorrow and acute sense of loss, because of certain truths I hold very strongly and most surely believe.

On the gravestone of my parents yonder in a Cheshire churchyard it says, 'Gone home with a Friend'. It says that because I had it put there because that is how I feel about them. He promised them a life with Him in His Father's house, and I know His promises are good and faithful and sure. Jesus Christ will never let you down.

Also, I know that none of those who love Jesus ever meet for the last time. My loved ones have just caught an earlier train, as it were, and later on I shall rejoin them.

So I can rejoice, because I know where they are. I shall see them again and, above all, I can rejoice because they are with Jesus. He said to those who love Him, 'I'm getting a place ready for you so that we can be together.' Now I don't need or want to know anything more about heaven than that – there's quite enough there to enable me to rejoice and to face the future unafraid and to leave the rest with Jesus.

A prayer to end:

Lord Jesus, increase my faith and hope and trust in you so that it is big enough for both here and hereafter.

AMEN

HOME FOR CHRISTMAS

Christmas – for very few of us is it all fun and games, all joy and jollity. For many it brings both sunshine and shadow – mixed memories. Yet I wonder what it was gave you most joy last time. Goodness knows, there's joy enough in celebrating the coming of Jesus Christ for any man, and that in itself brought me so much happiness again. But among the other events that go with the festival – what do you prize most now, on reflection? Was it a prime turkey like the man said? Did you get the wish you've been wanting for years? Shall you ever forget the children's faces when they opened their stocking at 6.30 a.m. – or was it 5.30? Did someone remember you thought would forget?

I had presents that meant so much to me. For all too short a time all my family were together under one roof and we ate a meal together – that was great. But I think what gave me most joy was a Christmas card I had – here is part of what it said: 'When I was down and out and came to your Mission, because of your sermon the other week I decided to try and make it back home to my wife and daughter. Thank you for what you did – and may the Mission go on and perhaps send another man home . . .'

Only a part of his wonderful message, but there's enough there to rejoice about. A man re-united with family and home because the gospel was preached. A man who is grateful, too, and a man who wants others to find out the same joy that came to him.

Time and time again I've read and re-read that Christmas card, because it reminds me, lest I tend to forget, that that is what the Church of Christ is all about – that is what is meant by evangelism. Joseph and Mary went home to Bethlehem the first Christmas that ever was, and the Christ child came to them there. So the business of the Church is that of calling men home – back to their Father's house – back to the presence of Jesus. In the end it has nothing to do with church buildings, church structures, church divisions, church committees – not even church VIPs, whoever they might be. It has to do with conversion, a new way, a rebirth – a fresh start with Jesus.

Well, now we're into a new year – a time of new beginnings and new birth all around us. So what better time than this for me to decide all over again, never to miss an opportunity to speak a good word for Jesus – never to let an opportunity go by for commending my Saviour to you. Never to lose the realities while I'm grasping bubbles.

Don't let this be for you a year on the perimeter –a year of almost but not quite, a year of sham and shoddy. Put your hand into the hand of Christ and tell Him you surrender ALL to Him – to His kingly rule of love. No half-measures, no timidity, no expediency – but wholeheartedly commit yourself to Him. I know no other way for you and me to be quite sure that this will be a blessed year for us. Can you promise this with me? This year I'm His, and only His, and He is mine, for ever and for ever. Can you – or perhaps I should ask, will you?

My prayer then is this – make it yours too:

Lord Jesus Christ, in full and glad surrender I yield my life to Thee for ever and ever.

AMEN

REFLECTORS

When I was a very young minister, the widow of a former missionary gave me amongst other things, a lantern slide projector. It was an amazing piece of apparatus – beautifully made in steel and brass. It worked off the mains electricity supply when she gave it to me, but it wasn't always so. She gave me everything that went with it, and it was plain for me to see that it had originally been constructed to work either from an oil lamp or else an acetylene carbide light. I remember even now, when I first saw it, thinking of that good man far away in the bush showing slides about Jesus and His parables to the natives. I wired it up to the mains and had an experimental run and was disappointed – the pictures were far from good, blurred and indistinct. A pity.

About the same time that I was given the projector, I was running a Jowett car of blessed memory. I still look back to that two-stroke motor car with affection. I christened it Dorcas after the woman in the Bible who was full of good works. It had one fault, and driving round those country lanes and along the river banks in East Yorkshire, it was a grievous fault – the headlights were very poor. Sometimes I really had to strike a match to see if they were on. However, this fault was soon put right. A pal of mine took one look and said, 'Ah – new reflectors – that's what she needs.' I got them, and my word, what a difference! Ever after that all was well.

It was then that I remembered my magic lantern too, and sure enough, when I got it out and examined it closely, the reflector on that was in very poor shape. I had it re-silvered, and for a long time I think that magic lantern gave a lot of joy to a lot of people.

The light was perfectly all right in both cases, but in both cases the reflectors were poor and faulty, and so the light shone feebly and ineffectively.

Right at the heart of the Christmas story is the fact that

Christ came to a dark world and He brought Light, and from then until now the darkness has never been able to put it out. It shines on. The lights on my magic lantern and my Jowett car were not out, they were still shining, but not as brightly nor as effectively as they should have been – or at least, not until the reflectors were renewed.

Jesus said He was the Light of the World, but He also said that His true followers were, too. They, or should I say, I am a reflector of Jesus in the world today. I have no light of my own to offer, but I can and I should be reflecting His light wherever I can.

Whenever men get only a dim or a blurred idea of what Jesus is like – whenever men lose their way in the darkness on their journey through life, it could well be that the reflectors are so poor that even His light is poor and dim. It could mean that I need to be renewed, repolished, made afresh, so that He – Jesus – not only shines on me with all the light of His wonderful love, but also that He shines from me so that others may come to know Him and to love Him and to journey safely. It seems to me that I have got to live very near to Him all the time – to be renewed, remade by Him all the time. To have Him remove all the dirt and scars and blemishes, so that in thought, word and deed I might truly reflect my Saviour – the Light of the World.

A prayer to end:

Shine upon me, O Lord, and make me so like You that I may reflect Your Light and Your Love to all men.

AMEN

ARTHUR'S COILS

My uncle had a brother-in-law named Arthur who as far as I recall, for he died early in my life, was always an invalid. I do not remember him except as a man who was house-fast, unable to go to work and suffering from what was always referred to as 'Arthur's complaint'. Even to this day I have not the slightest idea of what that complaint was.

I do recall, however, that he had some mysterious treatment – this treatment was always referred to as 'Arthur's coils'. It consisted of a box about an eight-inch cube and sticking out of one end was a handle and sticking out of the other end there were two lengths of wire. At the end of each wire there was, soldered on to the wire, a length of brass tubing about half an inch in diameter and four to five inches long. Now the treatment was for Arthur to hold the two copper handles and for someone to turn the box handle, which in some mysterious way generated electricity and the shocks it gave to him were supposed to do him good.

Fair enough – I'll never know just how much good they did him, but I do know it was a fascinating game to me and my cousins to have a go on Arthur's box, and to see how much of the shock you could stand – and my goodness, it really could give you a kick! We also discovered elaborations on the game. We found that two or even more could join hands, and then the one at one end of the row could hold one brass tube and the other at the other end could hold the other brass tube, and when someone turned the handle the shocks would pass through the lot of us until somebody couldn't stand it any more and let go of either someone's hand or the tube. Then the circuit was broken and that was the end of that. We had a lot of fun out of Arthur's box – even though, underneath, I think we were all a bit scared of it.

With Arthur's box the power was generated and it could pass through one person and be given to another. At Christmas, a lot of power was generated – for me it was the power of love, and it came to me, and through me and my few colleagues it was passed on to those who needed it so much. Gifts of money and food and clothing were generated out of the power of love in lots of people's hearts and sent to us and we stood between and passed them on to scores of folk in the East End who otherwise would have winter but no Christmas. We only completed the circuit – we were only the channels of God's grace and love.

The thing I've kept on saying to myself, is that this is not just something to remember and to bring out once a year with the holly and the mistletoe. This is a way of life for all time – this is the way of Jesus. Each day there come to us opportunities to bridge the gap between God and man. Each day there comes to us a chance to put one hand into the hand of Christ and our other hand into the hand of our fellow man – to pass on something of the power of Christ's love to those who are weak and helpless and sin-sick.

You see, I know so well that unless I have one hand in the hand of Christ, I have nothing to pass on to any man. But if I do hold fast to the hand of Christ, then all His love is really wasted until and unless that other hand of mine reaches out to my fellow man and I become the means whereby he comes to know my Lord and Saviour as His Lord and Saviour.

So my prayer to end this morning is for you and for me.

Use us, O Lord, to span the space between our fellows and Thy grace. Through Jesus Christ our Lord.

AMEN

UNNECESSARY

I'm not sure where the town in question was. What I am sure about is that it all began in a meeting of the Town Council, at which the Town Dadas began to compare their town's amenities with those of neighbouring towns. They well nigh regarded those neighbours as enemies, and civic pride was something of great import. The real problem was that they had not got a Town Hall, and towns nearby all had one.

At last the great decision was made, and architects were requested to submit plans. When they met to consider these, the one which pleased them most showed a spacious and splendid building. When they looked more closely, however, they noticed that it was a single span roof. It would be the Town Hall with the largest single span roof anywhere.

That started it – a very long debate. Was it safe? Crowds would gather there. Ought there not to be some pillars – say only four – but some pillars to take the weight of such a span of roof? In the end the architect was sent for and their doubts and fears put before him. Quietly and firmly he explained that he knew his job – that he had given due thought to all their fears and, based upon his professional calculations, the plans as submitted were quite safe and their fears were ungrounded.

The architect went away, but not so the debate. It went on and on. Twice the Council meeting was adjourned, and in the end they agreed to accept the plans but they must insist there be introduced into them four pillars to take the weight – to ensure the safety of all who would, down the years, use the Town Hall.

With a great deal of reluctance the architect agreed. The tenders came in, the building began. It was finished and duly and officially opened, and what a worthy occasion that opening day was! Right from the start nothing but praise was showered upon the new building except – just here and there and very quietly, mind you – the odd person did say how much better it would have been without the pillars, there were times when they would be a nuisance and a hindrance. However, 'a splendid Town Hall' was the general opinion.

I think it was over twenty years after the opening that by now a new set of Town Dadas met and decided it was high time the Town Hall was decorated. Tenders came in, one was accepted, and the scaffolding put up and the work began. A day or two after it started, the foreman painter climbed the scaffolding right up to the roof and when he came down, he simply said, 'Funny thing, but you know each of those four pillars is three inches from the roof. They need not be there at all, they don't carry anything.'

It will go a long way towards making your life a happy one if only you can sort out the things which really matter – those things which are really needed in life. So many things that so many people strive after are, in the end, quite useless and unnecessary. We could well do without them. I hope we will have the wisdom to know this.

A prayer:

Help me, O Lord, to know and to strive after only those things which in your sight belong to true life and also to life eternal.

AMEN

INFLATION CURED

A man went to his doctor and the doctor gave him a thorough examination and asked him lots of questions, and then he paused for quite a while and seemed quite lost. Then he looked at the man and said, 'Have you had this before?' 'Yes', he said. 'Well,' said the doctor, 'you've got it again!'

The thing I want to talk about now seems to me a bit like that – it's that thing called 'Inflation', and it seems ever with us. I grow more and more inclined to think that there is a tendency to look for the cure in the wrong place – I know this is true for me. Yet I don't go to my newsagent for two pork chops or to my chemist for new shoes, and I don't go to Euston Station to get a bus to Exeter. Mention inflation and we all think 'they' should solve it – the politicians – the economists – the oil sheiks – the great powers – the bosses – the unions – they should do something about it. I wonder.

I don't know if I'm even qualified to define inflation, but my simple mind does know that it has to do with things getting dearer to buy and yet we're not getting enough money to buy them. It has to do with outgoings rising and incomings standing still – or even in some cases getting less. All of which in the end adds up to somebody, somewhere having to do without something. Either those who supply must reduce their price or those who buy must get more to pay with or else, as I say, somebody, somewhere has got to do without.

Now here's the problem – just so long as I feel that that somebody somewhere is anybody anywhere but me, I don't see any real hope of solving the problem. I think it was one of the Presidents of the U.S.A. who had a plaque on his desk which said, 'The buck stops here'. To solve inflation I'm quite sure that is ultimately the only way – that the buck stops with me. It means I have at least to be satisfied with what I've already got, and it may mean I shall need to be content in the future with less than I have been accustomed to, and indeed, less then what I have come to regard as my rightful dues.

Now, I find this pill hard to swallow. I can think of a whole host of people who ought to be satisfied with less – a whole host of people who seem to me to be quite all right, thank you very much, and I want to say, 'Let's start with them'. But until the process touches me, not only those above and on a par with me but even those below – until then, we shall never really solve the problem.

I once read about a lifeboat going to sea to rescue a sole survivor lying on the deck of a fishing vessel broken on the rocks. The lifeboat got alongside and they got aboard the wreck and reached the injured man, and as they prepared to get him off the wreck and on to the lifeboat he pointed below deck and was just able to gasp out, 'There's another man.'

Yes, that's the way to solve inflation – that's the way of Jesus, because He said that when we spoke to God we were to call Him Father, and when you do that, then that other man is your brother and you can't let him perish, can you? Yes – I know that's the way to solve inflation. So, in prayer, I say:

Father God, may my greed never cause my brother to be in need. For Your Son's sake.

AMEN

. . . IN THE HIGH ST.

Some of the biggest changes in my lifetime from the point of view of a parson have been the changes which have taken place regarding Sunday. My mother used to tell me, 'Better a man had never been born than Sunday shod and Sunday shorn.'

We had no Sunday papers, no games, no knitting, a minimum of work and only very selected reading. Well, most of that has gone, and it is not my intention to evaluate the change – sufficient to say in passing that many of the replacements are far worse than the originals. The emphasis I want to make is this. While I am second to no man in agreeing to 'remember the Sunday to keep it holy', I want to stress the value and importance of 'remembering the week-day to keep it holy.'

I'm thinking of week-days as work days, and I believe it is both sound and necessary today to say, and say over and over again, that if ever there was a need for stressing that our work can and should be done to the glory of God it is now. Like the rest of mankind, a Christian must work to earn his daily bread and maintain his family. But he works also for a higher motive and under different pressures than those of fear, insecurity and greed. He works for the good of men and the glory of God, and in so doing he finds a satisfaction not to be derived from earthly rewards or diminished by earthly hardships. So I say Monday can be as significant and sacred as Sunday. Whatever we do as our work should be done to the glory of God.

I began thinking like this when I remembered hearing about a church that had an illuminated sign made to shine outside the church with a Christian message for the season of Advent. It was made, erected and switched on and it looked really good. Passers-by were all able to read it and it read, 'Glory to God in the Highest.' They were very proud of it in the church concerned, and lots of folk commended them on what they had done.

Then, as often happens with these electrical gadgets, the gremlins got in and the result was the letter E in HIGHEST failed to light up. Hasty arrangements were made to have it repaired, when some wise soul said, – 'No, – leave it as it is – – it's even nearer now to the message of Christmas.' So they left it, and it shone out now and read, 'Glory to God in the High St.'

How wise they were to leave it – how truly it told the Christmas story. A story of a God who left the Throne of Heaven and became a baby, the Christ child, to dwell with men – men and women, boys and girls – in the High Street, in the everyday places. Not just a God of Heaven, and altar, and church, and Sundays, but a God of hearth and homes and hearts of workmen, not just of Kings and priests and palaces. The visit He paid, which was the life of God in Christ here below, ended one day and He went back again to the side of God the Father, but He left a handful of ordinary folk still down here to go on living to His glory in the High Street; and countless thousands of such folk have gone on doing it ever since. Sunday is a special day for them when they celebrate His victory – but on weekdays, too, we should be living our lives to His glory.

A prayer to end:

At all times, and in all places, help us to bring glory and honour to Your name.

AMEN

PRAYERS

In my early years as a boy growing up in a Christian home and in the Methodist Church, one of the things which I now realise I took for granted was that ordinary Christian folk were extraordinarily good at praying. Down the years I often heard my Dad saying his prayers – indeed I could repeat some of those prayers now. Then at the chapel – not only the ministers and lay preachers but lots of others of humble station – salt-makers, lumpmen, postmen, housewives, teachers, platelayers – yes, lots of them could pray. I don't think it was ever easy for them so to do, but it did seem natural. You didn't have to be a special person, in a special place, dressed up in special clothes, with a special book in order to talk to that someone whom they usually referred to as a Loving Heavenly Father.

One of the grandest things about my father was that I could always talk to him, knowing he would listen, and knowing too that he would answer and that that answer would be good and true, and what he felt was the best answer for me – yes, even if sometimes it hurt, sometimes it was a refusal or even a condemnation. So, as I think back, my Methodist fore-elders talked to their Heavenly Father. There seemed to be nothing in between them and Him, no let or hindrance except their sins, and these they told Him about and left Him to deal with them and to tell them what to do next. They were not struggling to get through. They were not fighting to gain contact. They were not arguing nor debating, they were talking, and also from time to time they took jolly good care to listen.

Yes, as I say, so much of that I took for granted, and it is only with the passing of many years that I have come to know that such a facility in their prayers was not arrived at overnight. They were what they were because of much practice. Prayer was regular and it had a fixed place in their lives, like eating and sleeping. Prayer for them was not a sort of optional extra, nor was it ever a panic last resort. The language they used was as simple as their faith and had a beauty all of its own, but above everything else it was personal stuff – man to man. There were no vague generalities – no random ramblings.

I remember telling my father once that there were times when I didn't know what to say in my prayers and asking him if ever he felt like that. I was shattered when he said he did. 'Well, what do you say then?' I asked him. 'Why lad,' he said, 'I just tell Him I don't know what to say and I don't know what to ask and will He please tell me and He always does.'

The late Dr Sangster once told in my hearing of a dear lady who was passing through a very rough passage in her life – it seemed to be tumbling in around her, and somebody asked her how she went on saying her prayers under such circumstances. 'Oh! I just say, "No questions Lord – only Amens."'

Are you keeping your prayer life in good repair? If your life is such that you are too busy to pray, then that simply means that you are too busy. I want you to know that no matter how life is for you, you can speak to God about it. 'What a privilege to carry everything to God in prayer.' – Are you enjoying that privilege to the full? If not, why not?

Our prayer is the prayer of those first disciples:

Lord, teach us how to pray.

AMEN

WORDPASSERS

It was a Methodist minister who introduced me as a boy to Tom Sawyer and Huckleberry Finn – it was the Rev. J. E. Dark, and I've always been grateful. Yet, strange though it may seem, I didn't know until recently that Mark Twain's real name was Samuel Langhorne Clemens, and I learned how he got the name Mark Twain. Sam had an ambition to be a steamboat pilot on the Mississippi River – and he served an apprenticeship for two years. There were times when a man called the leadsman kept casting a weighted line over the side of the ship, and when he felt it touch the bottom he was able to tell the depth of the water. This was a vital piece of information for the pilot, especially in the most hazardous stretches of the river. The leadsman would cry out his sounding: 'Mark Three – Quarter-less-three – Half Twain – Quarter Twain – Mark Twain – Mark Twain' – and this was the source from which Sam got his name which he used in his writings.

But when I was reading that I came across another piece of information, quite new to me, and it made me think. When the leadsman was sounding the depths in storms and hurricanes, even if he'd shouted at the top of his voice, his voice would not have carried to the bridge, and so a special arrangement was made. The cries – the soundings of the leadsman – were passed from the hurricane deck to the man at the helm by men who were especially appointed to be 'wordpassers' – men whose job it was to pass on the truth which was given to them in order that those truths might be used to preserve the lives of others. If they failed to listen – if they passed on wrong information – then the lives of many were in dire peril. Have you ever heard of these wordpassers, I wonder?

I've always been glad and grateful that certain truths were handed to me when I was a lad. My parents, teachers, friends, preachers, told me over the years some of those eternal verities about Jesus and His love – about life and death, about here and hereafter, good and bad, sin and salvation. I listened and, do you know, with the passing of the years I never found any good reason to doubt them or reject them. If and when things haven't worked out in my life, it has never been because those early wordpassers in my life told me something false, but always – yes always – the fault has been mine.

I've always been glad too that I heard the call of God to be a wordpasser – a Methodist preacher. I wouldn't have been anything else for anything in the world. All my life I've tried to pass on what was given to me in my early days – that word about Jesus, the Word who became flesh, became what we are so that we could become what He is.

To go back for a moment to Mark Twain – they must have needed more wordpassers, and fully dedicated ones, when the boat was in storm and hurricane. I want you and me to remember that in these days. It has never been more important than it is today that I should listen very intently to what Jesus has to say to me, and that I should be more dedicated than ever in passing on that word to others – to you.

A prayer to end this morning:

Lord, speak to me that I may speak in living echoes of Thy tones.

AMEN

LIQUIDITY PROBLEMS

I have heard so much about it over recent months that even I have begun to use it – even though I'm still not sure what it means. Very frequently where I work I am approached by someone to lend them a pound; and you know full well that if you obliged you would never see your pound again, and you would never see the person who prefaced his plea with such a summary of your character that you felt almost cannonised. I've often replied to such cries of the heart – or more often thirst – by saying, 'Well now, I only have one pound which I lend out and at the moment it's out, but if and when it comes in again I'll lend it to you!' But recently I've hidden behind a more modern piece of jargon and I've said, 'Sorry, I've got a *liquidity* problem.' Yes the word is being bandied about and is, we are told, at the very heart and core of the present day problems of industry. Be that as it may, I think there are liquidity problems in the world today about which we should all be concerned, and in the solving of which a great deal could and should be done.

As someone who has never, never been hungry, I am much bothered about the hungry half of the world, and I know that very much of it is caused in certain parts by something which is a liquidity problem and is generally referred to as *drought.* Too little liquid – too little water. What bothers me here may be due to my all too simple mind, but when in this age of technology man is virtually performing miracles, I am at a loss to know why so much inventiveness and ingenuity cannot contrive ways and means of moving water to where it's needed and when it's needed. I'm sure that in so doing he would be far better employed than in many of his contemporary pursuits.

Or take the folk I live and work with. So many of them have a liquidity problem. They cannot get enough – they long for, fight for, steal and cheat and lie for alcohol in one form or another – even in the last resort the metal polish or surgical spirits on our premises if they can lay their hands on them. Now here's a real liquidity problem.

When we discover the source of what kills a man in medicine we deal with it there – at source. It's better, we know, to eliminate the cause of typhoid, tuberculosis, leprosy, than to wait until we have to cure it. Believing that smoking is harmful, we've taken a modest step and folk are warned. Yet we do know the cause of alcoholism – of all the increasing ills and hurts and evils that go with drinking – yet no one bothers, it seems, to deal with it at source. No one says, 'In the making of it – in the brewery – you are making hell, not only for the increasing numbers who actually drink it, but for as many more, among them all too often little children, who suffer or die annually because of this liquidity problem.' This problem seems to me a vital one. It's eroding away the fibre of our nation, it's far more serious than all the problems of industry, and yet it is largely and expediently ignored.

A prayer:

Open our eyes to see and our mouth to speak whenever evil rears its ugly head, O Lord.

AMEN

CHIDDINGFOLD GLASS

For two folk born and bred in the country and now living in the East End of London, it is a particular joy and pleasure to have an opportunity to go back again to rural England. This we were able to do when we spent a glorious week-end in the parish of Chiddingfold on the borders of Surrey and Sussex with our good friends the Rector and his lady. I also shared in the Harvest Festival Services and in all was blessed and refreshed in more ways than one.

It is a moving experience to walk through the lych-gate with its coffin-rest and to recall that you are walking on ground which may well have been consecrated and set apart as holy for more than a thousand years. There are so many memories I would like to share with you, but one will have to suffice. I want to tell you about the West window.

Let me begin by telling you that once upon a time, from about 1226 to 1626, glass was being made there in the lovely village. But none of it remained in the village. It went far and wide – maybe to Winchester, Westminster and even York Minster. When I say none of it remained, that's hardly true. A former curate of the church, helped by his family, discovered on local farmland the sites of three separate glass furnaces. They found 427 fragments of original Chiddingfold glass and over half of these bits and pieces were coloured. One piece has been dated as not later than 1325, and much of it was made between 1450 and 1550. Well, all these bits and pieces were used as they were found. With no cutting and shaping, they were leaded together to form the West window and the completed window was, most fittingly, dedicated to the memory of the glass-makers of Chiddingfold and others connected locally with the industry.

I like that, and I'm glad I gained this knowledge through my visit to the country. I like to think of all those scrapped, rejected, lost bits and pieces being gathered up and carefully fitted together until the result was a thing of beauty and a joy for ever.

I like to think of it because so often it seems that round and about there are lots and lots of folk doing seemingly little and almost meaningless acts of good, of kindness, of caring and sharing, and they seem sometimes to get lost under the weight and welter of evil things in these days. All too often it seems that the old hymn was right when it spoke of 'right being on the scaffold and wrong being on the throne'. Noise and publicity clang out in strident notes an almost continuous blare of bad sinful things being done; yet, alongside, there are these other deeds – deeds of love and mercy – things that are beautiful, lovely, honest and of good report. I like to think like that because in my heart I know that Jesus, who Himself had the hands of a craftsman, is picking them all up – not one is ever lost, I'm sure – and bit by bit, in His good time, He's making a pattern in a part of what He calls His Kingdom. When it's made, and the light of His love shines through it, we shall see and know that it was all worth while, for somewhere in all the scores of pieces there's sure to be a place for my bit and for your bit. And it's not merely for centuries, it's for eternity.

Our prayer to end asks:

Let us never grow weary in well doing, Lord Jesus. Fit our offerings into your great pattern, for Your name's sake.

AMEN

JOB SATISFACTION

As a rule, when we meet and ask one another, 'How are you?' we get an equally commonplace reply; and we are hardly aware that we have enquired and even less aware of the reply. At odd times, however, there are folk who do not reply in conventional terms. Mary, in my home town, used to say, 'I am as I am and I can't be any amerer,' – whatever that might have meant. And John, who lived in the same place, had his special answer and he used to say, 'I'm still walking about – it saves funeral expenses.'

Another reply I've come across in many different parts of the country is one I'm sure you've heard, even if you have not used it – 'I'm overworked and underpaid'. I sat and turned over in my mind the folk I've known who used that reply, and as far as my memory serves me, it was never true for them. In not one solitary case were they either overworked or underpaid. For you see, those for whom it is true, for one reason or another never say so. If they were the kind of person who would say so, well, they just wouldn't stick it out in the kind of job they are doing – they would have been up and off long ago.

I was more than thrilled a while ago when a rare and refreshing breeze blew across the football scene. For too long now, we who love football, and have done for many years, have been watching the sad sagas unfold of discontent, disruption, disloyality – and many of us have grown more and more disenchanted. In case after case it has seemed to those of us looking in from the outside that, as the song says, money is the root of all evil. Now – as I said – a new, fresh, warm breeze has blown and we have heard with delight of someone who didn't want more money, didn't want more fame, but preferred to stay in a humbler set-up with youngsters. Who spoke of a debt he felt he owed because of past kindness. Who, even though he was not tied down by any contract, still said, 'Here I stay', and went on to tell of the value he placed on a happy home and family life and what he called 'job satisfaction'.

I'm sure that he had that deep satisfaction in the main because he gave little or no thought either to reward or number of hours worked. Because he was doing something he felt to be worthwhile, those lesser things never loomed large enough to spoil his happiness.

My lady colleague at Whitechapel is a Wesley Deaconess. I don't know anyone who could more justly claim that, during all her ministry, she has been overworked and underpaid, but – she'll never forgive me for telling you about it – because she too has job satisfaction, payment and hours never enter her head.

Part of the teaching of Jesus was to tell us not to be over-anxious about THINGS – and to tell us that, if and when we followed Him, life would be abundantly satisfying. I have found that to be true as and when I have taken him at His word. Having more and working less is not the guaranteed royal road to satisfaction. Giving more and serving more, especially serving Jesus, is. So I end as I began and ask you – How are you?

Lord Jesus, whenever anybody asks me how I am, may I be able to reply that I am happy to be Your obedient servant. For Your name's sake.

AMEN

UNDER NEW MANAGEMENT

Somebody asked me the other day, if I had to live on only one thing – what would I choose. Well, you think about it – what would you select? Chops, cockles, caviare, cauliflower, crackers? For me, I decided it would be a close thing between cheese and pork-pies, but I think in the end I should come down on the latter. Yes, pork-pies for me – real ones, mind you!

When I was in theological college I found it necessary to supplement the food I was given, and often resorted to pork-pies. But there was one pie shop which I passed regularly and I never once went in. You see, the window was not only full of pies, it was usually full of flies as well, and the whole set-up had a dirty appearance – most off-putting, in spite of my bias towards the goods which they offered.

I was passing by one day, and all the front window was whitewashed over. I peered inside and saw that the whole of the interior had been gutted and a couple of workmen were busily engaged inside doing something or other. Just over a couple of weeks later I passed again. My goodness, what a transformation! The window all cleaned, the inside bright and shiny, customers going in and coming out, lovely pies in the window, no flies, and a gay strip poster across the window said, 'Under New Management.'

Needless to say, I became a very regular customer after that – in fact, I should think I very nearly qualified to be classed as a shareholder. You see, it made all the difference in the world once the establishment was under new management.

It's not too far a cry, I hope, to jump from pork-pies to Parliament, because there we've got a new management. Oh! I know it's the same party as last time, but it is a new government, and what I want to say would be equally true if any of the other parties had got in this last time.

What I want to say is this – that in the end, the full and real answer to our problems of flies and pies may well be met by a new management, but the problems of the nation and, indeed, your problems and mine, will never be solved by a new government. What I need, and what you need, is not a new government but a New Governor. Our lives need to come under new management. Just so long as I govern, just so long as I rule, just so long as self is on the throne of my life, then there is inevitably trouble – inevitably there will be some squalor, some dirt, something uninviting in the shop window. Things like greed and envy and jealousy and coveting, grasping and grabbing – all these things creep in and spoil the display we call our lives if we ourselves are ruling. I have found that, when Christ becomes Governor and I live under His government, then under that New Management I can by His grace and guidance begin to offer something winsome and winning and attractive to other people. It was so pronounced in those early followers of Jesus, that they turned the world upside-down. We could and should do that, and we will do – not with a change of government, but with a change of Governor.

Our prayer to end, then:

Lord Jesus Christ, so rule in our hearts that our lives will show forth Thy praise.

AMEN

FOUR-LETTER WORDS

Ever since a certain court case some years ago now we have had a very odd usage of a couple of simple words, so that folk refer sometimes to 'four letter words,' and the accepted interpretation is that the said words are what are otherwise called dirty words. I don't see why you should call any word dirty, but I know full well it's what the word means or describes that is felt to be dirty. We could argue for ever about what is dirty and what is not. What I want to say is that I grow very fearful when what were once honourable, clean and wholesome words, become dirty, and when what were dirty words become accepted as good and clean. Enough about words in general, here's what I'm getting at.

There was a day not too long ago when that four-letter word WORK meant for the vast majority of people, something noble and good and praiseworthy and had about it a certain dignity. I found recently a long-handled soft brush about an inch wide and a piece of brass about three inches by eight, with a slit up the middle. This was my father's button stick and brush – into the slot he placed the metal buttons on his uniform and polished them regularly. It didn't make him any better a railway signalman, but because he was proud of the job which he did – for little enough pay, too – he always kept his uniform well groomed. He insisted on having his proper rest, in being on time – he was late twice in forty-two years – and at his job he gave his uttermost as he saw it, to preserve the regular and safe running of trains. He did not feel it was debasing and servile to be a public servant. On the contrary, work for him was not a dirty word. – it was a clean, noble thing even though it meant anti-social hours – rarely a week-end or a Sunday off, going to work when most folk were going to bed. Yes, I say it's a pity that there is this tendency to imply that work is a dirty word.

On the other hand, there's this process in reverse. In those earlier days of my life there was a dirty word of four letters –

nothing to do with sex or bodily organs or functions. It was the word DEBT. I'm not speaking of unavoidable debt – this I know about and accept. No, I'm speaking of debt deliberately incurred in obtaining something you don't have to have – something you want, rather than something you need. Debt incurred to enable someone to put on a show of possession or apparel or pursuit. Debt that takes the place of patience and thrift. Debt because of a base sense of values. Then I hold that debt is a dirty word; yet so many folk are not the slightest bit bothered – after all, they argue, THEY, whoever they are, should do something about it – more grants, more and more benefits, more wages.

I've always been glad that Jesus grew up in the home of a carpenter and that He worked. The hands through which the nails went were a craftsman's hands, and honest work is Christlike. I'm sad when I recall He had no possessions, but I would have been sadder if He had had a lot and never paid for them. Yes, I think WORK is a clean word and DEBT is a dirty one – both four letters.

Dear God, renew in our day a sense of the dignity of honest work and a healthy fear of dishonest debt. For Christ the Carpenter's sake.

AMEN

THE ROAD-SWEEPER

I keep hearing the expression 'job-satisfaction' these days, and I suppose I have a great deal to be thankful for that I have a job I would never change – indeed, I never cease to be amazed that in a sense I get paid for doing what I want to do more than anything else in the world.

I knew a man in a Midlands city who was an honours graduate of Oxbridge and his life had tumbled in and his own mental stability had been in jeopardy for some time. Of his brilliance there was no doubt, and of his utter misery there was even less. He eventually got a job, and believe it or not he became a road-sweeper – no, more than that, he became a happy and contented road-sweeper. He told me it gave him a thrill and peace of mind to look back over what he came to call his road and to see it swept clean and tidy. As far as I know, he's still doing his road sweeping and in it he gets this thing called job-satisfaction.

Fair enough, but it can't be like that for the poor fellow who sweeps the road we look out on to where I live. I wonder his mental stability isn't impaired. You see, always, night and day, there are motor cars parked in that street outside our premises, and all the poor man can ever do is to sweep the bits of spaces in between the cars and to leave the rest hidden away inaccessible underneath all the parked cars. The end result is a clean bit, a dirty bit, a clean bit and a dirty bit, occurring so frequently that really it means we have always got a dirty street – always we must look out on to filth and mess. Well, there's not much we can do about that – I rather doubt it would alter matters even if we resolved to stop paying any rates. So we put up with it and hope something will turn up, which thing I doubt very much.

I've stood at the window looking at the road-sweeper many times and felt sorry for him. But more than that, I've thought, 'That's what I do' – and I suspect it's what you do.

In our lives we tend to keep clean all those places that are to be seen and which can be readily got at. We want to give folk the impression that our lives are sweet and clean and beyond reproach, so where it shows we brush up, we keep it tidy – splendid! There are still the other parts – the hidden, obscure, hard-to-get-at parts. What is it like there in your life? A lad in that transition stage from short to long trousers was told by his mother to get a wash. 'Which trousers am I putting on?' he asked. 'Why?' said his mother. 'I want to know if I need to wash my knees!' he replied.

Jesus was quite insistent that it is cleanliness – goodness – in those inner hidden parts which matters most. It was no good, according to Him, being clean and whitewashed outside. His Father God wasn't looking there anyway, He was looking deep inside. Is the same purity, whiteness, goodness to be found there? I find it easiest to be like the roadman and to tidy up the visible. Yet I know, and I'm sure that you do too, that that is not enough. Christ wants us and is willing to help us to be clean and good, through and through.

So my prayer to end is:

Good Lord, so dwell in my heart and life that what is not seen is as truly Your image as what is seen, for Your name's sake.

AMEN

WINDOW BOXES

I was saying recently that there were some things I had missed in life because I was a Methodist minister and because from time to time, we moved house and moved to another circuit. Amongst those things – and they are very few, I might add – is this. I would have liked to have had a greenhouse. I think the propagating side of gardening would have given me a great deal of satisfaction. I could have got a real thrill out of pottering about under glass, as it were, and raising plants from seeds.

Still, there are modest things to be done without a greenhouse. Where I live in Whitechapel Road, is not renowned for its flowers and gardens – we tend to see them only on the stalls – but here and there and yonder you do come across the odd window box. Around the outside of my church mission we have got about half a dozen or so such window boxes. This year we were given a few geranium plants and they have done very well indeed. I've been so pleased with them that a Saturday or two ago I decided to take some cuttings. I have struck about twenty of these, and now I can only hope they will take so that next year we can have an even better show in the summer. In the spring, we are hoping we shall have some daffodils again. I've noticed that many, many folk pause as they pass our premises and they look pleased to see the colour and the beauty of our few flowers. So, apart from giving us who live here a deal of joy, I'm more than sure that they also give pleasure to other people.

Well, I'm no Percy Thrower, and we don't measure our plot in square yards, never mind acres; but we do the very best we can with the bit we've got to make it brighter, lovelier and more colourful.

All of which reminded me of a few lines from a hymn I used to sing in my Sunday School days: 'In this world of darkness, so we must shine, you in your small corner and I in mine'. It's a certain fact we are not going to throw our gardens open to the public. We can't have an Open Day and expect the crowds. Our bit, as I've implied, would go in the boot of a big motor car. But I hold it to be more than worth while to have planted ten daffodils or twenty geraniums in the East End of London in these days.

The longer I live, the more I find that lots and lots of folk are passing through dark days for one reason or another. Oh, I know sometimes it's their own fault. But what an opportunity for you and me to bring a bit of light and colour to their lives! That lonely shut-in old lady up the road from you and that crippled young fellow don't want – first and foremost – another five pounds a week. They want you to call and have a cup of tea and a chat and to deliver the sports paper perhaps every Saturday night.

Forget-me-nots are nice flowers to plant anywhere. If, there isn't a flower called forgiveness, well there ought to be and Jesus said we ought to be planting them in clusters of 490 – seventy times seven. It would make a big difference to a lot of homes and families and neighbourhoods if you would begin today to do just that. You in your small corner and I in mine could be, and should be, as conspicuous in our doing what Jesus would do as I'm hoping my geraniums will be again next summer.

A prayer to end:

Send us out today, O Father, resolved to leave this world with more colour and beauty in it before we return home tonight. For Jesus Christ's sake.

AMEN

RACHAEL

Those of us in this life who like me are Methodist ministers, belong to what is sometimes called an itinerant ministry – which does not mean, as one wag once suggested to me, that we are a 'shifty lot', but it does mean that every so often we change our place of abode and move to another circuit – could be north, south, east or west.

Like many other things, this has its joys and also its sorrows. I suppose they come out about even in the normal span of a forty years' ministry. I've missed having my own house and tinkering about with it as I chose. I've missed putting down roots. I've known the problems of our children's schooling, and we now have the fact of being quite a long way from our grandchildren. Yet, we find even this has its compensations, because, my goodness, we do get a real kick on all those occasions when by one means or another we do manage to see them.

Perhaps all this is why we got an extra bonus to the main part of our holiday this year in having one half of our family able to share it with us, and especially to see a little girl of just over one year old all day, every day, for a fortnight. I reckon it's a silly thing to do, but I sat one night trying to think if there was one word which I would use to describe her. The lovely north country word 'bonny' is as good as any, I should think, and yet the word I'm going to use is the word 'contentment'. I've never known such a contented child – and how I wish I were only half as contented! I think she's fortunate enough to have contented parents, and no doubt that helps, but I do pray most earnestly that as she grows up in this present age she will be able, even though the odds are all against her so doing, to preserve this spirit of contentment. What a lot of folk there are who are coveting for themselves other than what they have got, not because they really need it but because somebody else has got it; only to find that, when they have got that, whatever it is, then there's something else that someone else has, and that's coveted until it's acquired – and so on *ad infinitum.*

According to the tenth commandment it's a bad thing, and I always have a feeling of guilt whenever I go into a house with a genuine brass warming pan or a grandfather clock, because I always break that tenth commandment! To be serious, I'm not pleading for a dull, drab satisfaction that makes us little better than a door mat and just putting up with second best right down the line. No, what I'm trying to say is, if true joy and happiness are not to be found in this, then I hold that neither shall we find them in this and that. Or to use St Paul's words, 'I have learned in whatsoever state I am therewith to be content.' If it's bread and cheese for tea, be content, don't spoil the taste of it because they are having caviare next door. There are a lot more folk also having bread and cheese, and they are far more likely to share it with you if you haven't any than the far fewer folk with caviare.

Perhaps the real secret of my grand-daughter's contentment is because as yet she's an only child and not even aware of those things that someone else has got. Yet I still hope, as she grows up and does become aware of these things, she may still be able to avoid the sin of covetousness. I hope she will come to know and love Jesus and that He will be the only other person she will ever strive to keep up with. I hope this because I know that if only I would be contented so to live, only so can I ever really be contented.

So we end with a prayer:

Make me more interested in what I can give than in what I can get; more satisfied with what I've got than anxious because I want; more and more ready to learn that true life and joy do not consist of the abundance of things in my possession. Through Jesus Christ our Lord.

AMEN

SHEEP DOG TRIALS

Until last month I had only heard about them, read about them or seen an odd fleeting glimpse of such events on the television. Always I had hoped one day to see them properly, and even more I hoped that when I did I would know what was happening, and what was supposed to be happening, so that I could at least watch intelligently. For a dog-lover like me is bound to have more than a passing interest in sheep-dog trials.

Well, all those wishes of mine were fulfilled in one fell swoop last month – it was truly a fell swoop, for it all happened among the glory of the fells, in the very northern part of Lancashire. I went to preach in a lovely little village chapel (with a clean modern notice board and a well kept garden frontage – all other chapels please note) and I stayed with a farmer who not only runs dogs, but has actually won the International Trials in recent years. What finer guide could any man have had than that?

On the Saturday I saw my friend Harry (for the benefit of all sheep-dog folk, it was Light Harry not Black Harry) run his two dogs, Coon and Roy, at two trials. As I saw them and other dogs I was, in the words of one of our hymns, 'lost in wonder, love and praise'. How on earth a man standing still can control and guide a dog so that it can control and guide three sheep – starting about the length of six football pitches away – has to be seen to be believed. And it's all done by whistles, bless me! Sit down, stay, go to the right, now to the left, now forward – until in the end the sheep have covered the set course, come through three gateways and are penned up in a pen made by four gates forming a square.

I shall never forget that lovely afternoon in the fells and I've promised myself to see them again and again. One man and his dog – miraculous. How does it know left from right, and how do you pick out a whistle to sit down, one third of a mile away? There were always lots and lots of dogs about –

why didn't they all respond to all the whistles of all the shepherds? Why didn't they start running around after each other, and what do you do when three sheep all run off in different directions? Well, Harry and his pals know the secrets of these things. I only admired the results.

But my week-end in the fells brought me nearer to Jesus in so many ways – not least at these sheep-dog trials. After all, it takes a bit of accepting when Jesus says that sheep know the shepherd's voice and the shepherd knows his sheep individually – can any man and any animal have a relationship as close as that? Well, now I know they can. I've watched it and seen it – a relationship so close that the dog is a sort of extension of the will and work of his master; they are in tune with one another.

Now that, says Jesus to you and to me, is how we ought to be. Trained in His school of disciplined love, we who follow Him and name His name, should be extensions of His work and witness below. In thought, word and deed, we should be responding to our Master – running the course He intends, surmounting all the obstacles and arriving safely to where He is and hearing him say, 'Well done, good and faithful servant!'

A prayer then to end:

We are glad, Lord Jesus, that even from what we call dumb animals we can learn something of Your great and eternal gospel.

AMEN

OIL PAINTING

I only do it on holidays, and I get so much joy out of it that I always say to myself, 'Now I really must find time to keep this up, even if only in a modest kind of way, and not ignore it altogether for another year.' Well, this year I had another go – a go, that is at painting in oils – and I ended up with my impression of the Dovey estuary. Good, bad, fair, who am I to judge, and anyway who cares? I get a great deal of joy and relaxation out of the very doing of it.

Once you begin, it grows on you, and I find a very real fascination in trying to get just the right colour for this and that and also in finding new colours even in the sky and sea or a field, just because I'm looking very carefully and trying to reproduce them. I make some awful messes, and there must be lots of times when my wife looks over my shoulder and says, 'Mm – not bad,' when she really means, 'What on earth's that?' But, you see, it doesn't really matter too much because always I can start again. When I decide there's nothing of worth there – nothing I want to preserve – I just make a new start. No matter how badly I've done, how wrong it all is, I've always got plenty of white and can paint the lot out and make a completely fresh start on a bright white board and have another go at producing something that is worthwhile and which might give me some lasting joy and happiness. To an amateur like me, it's worth a great deal to know that at any given moment I may decide I can wipe out all that's been done and make a new beginning.

I don't think there is a week goes by in Whitechapel that we don't have someone – and often a lot of folk – tell us in one way or another they wish they could wipe out the past and begin again with a clean sheet. But I don't have to have men come to me and tell me this, because I myself know what it's like to feel like that, and I'm quite sure you do too. If only – if only – we could start all over again, with the previous and maybe present mess which we have made wiped out – if only.

But, you know, there's no 'if only' about it. We can and we should do just that. It was to make sure that you and I understood this enormous truth that God came here to be like us in Jesus Christ. In order to tell every man on earth that – no matter what kind of dark black mess he had made on the canvas of his life – through Jesus he can have all the mess wiped out and he can become a new person and begin all over again to paint a new and lovelier picture.

Perhaps you have made a bad or sad mess, and it's staring you in the face and it all seems so hopeless and quite beyond being altered – or as I might say, beyond redemption. Well, let me tell you, if you think that, you couldn't be further from the truth. You can begin again – you can start afresh with all your past mess blotted out, for the grand and simple reason that Jesus said so.

Let's tell Him about it:

Lord Jesus – it has been so easy to blotch up the canvas of my life and to have produced something I'm ashamed to see now. Take it all and wipe it out with your Love, and then guide my heart and hand so that I may produce a masterpiece – a piece like my Master would have it.

AMEN

'PUT LOVE FIRST'

Living as I do right in the heart of the East End of London, I have found it to be a bigger thrill than ever to spend a few days at the seaside. Because of this I was even more grateful to our kind friends who loaned us their bungalow because it had what was for me a very special virtue. You could stay at home there on the foulest of days and sit indoors and still look out from your armchair and see the sands, the sea shore, the Dovey estuary and the Welsh coast and far, far out to sea. I found it a real tonic, and I found myself sitting there for hours on end just watching. It seemed to have a special fascination, even after darkness had fallen.

While the general view was a benediction in itself, there were also special features. It was a splendid and popular place for sailing, and quite frequently when I looked out to sea, there they were sailing to and fro – sometimes at a fair rate of knots, sometimes becalmed, and once or twice blown right over.

Well, obviously I had little else to do but watch, sitting there – except of course I could think as well and so I did, quite often. One of the things that came to my mind was this. Those sailing boats really only move effectively for two reasons. Obviously they move when the wind blows – their sails billow out and away they go. Or else they move when driven along by the strength of the tide or the currents. And yet it is quite impossible to see the wind, or the tide or the currents as such – to look at these not inconsiderable means of power.

It's all too easy for you and me to get caught up today into the general belief that visible things matter most; indeed, some would go so far as to say that only seeing is believing, and they even doubt the sanity of anybody who puts their trust in anything or anybody unseen. Sitting there watching the dinghies and thinking, I recalled that our good friends whose bungalow it was have a son and his family in Canada –

across yonder, I thought, looking westward out to sea – and it's by something unseen that in a flash, as they sit where I was sitting, and their thoughts and their love cross the whole Atlantic and enfold their loved ones far away; and their love comes back in return. All quite invisible, but the strength of such love could rule the world.

Which only leads me on to say that I believe Paul was right when he said that in this world he knew about three things which last for ever – faith, hope and love, and the greatest of them all was love. After he said that he went on to say, 'Put love first.' That's what I want to do – that's what I want you to do. All day and every day – never rely upon those seemingly big things just because you can see them, but remember to put love first in every situation. It is still the greatest thing in the world.

Let's end with a prayer:

Lord Jesus, increase my faith so that even I may remove mountains. Enlarge my hope so that it reaches beyond time to eternity, and so fill me with love that my faith shall only be in Thee and my hope only to be with Thee for ever more.

AMEN

OUT PATIENTS

You can pick up some very deep truths and you can learn some very profound lessons in some very odd places. I say this is true because it's happened to me many times and it happened again quite recently.

I was sitting in the waiting room of the out-patients' department of the great London Hospital. Sitting next to me was an eastern gentlemen – quite young and very shy and very quiet. We did, however, begin to chat, and I discovered he had come along as company for a friend and fellow-countryman of his who – just then while I was talking to him – was actually in seeing one of the doctors. He was just waiting there for him to come out and then presumably to take him home.

Another doctor came out of another consulting room. He looked rather worried and went and spoke to the sister and a nurse, and then the nurse looked at this young chap sitting next to me and asked him, 'Do you speak Bengali?' and he said, 'Yes'. Well, the outcome was that he went in and acted as translator for some patient who could hardly speak English at all. You know, it could well be that he was the means of saving someone's life.

On my way home I thought – here was a man suddenly called on to speak his home language in what could have been a matter of life and death. Suppose – just suppose – you and I are called upon to speak a languge – the Christian language – to speak a good word for Jesus to someone. How would you get on? I'm not making a plea for all Christians to be preachers – God forbid! What I am saying is that there come to all of us opportunities to say a word on behalf of our faith, to speak out for truth, to announce where we stand in these days of declining standards and false and evil values. I look back on my years before I was a minister and I can recall a lot of men on the railway and in industry who were unashamed to stand up for their faith – who didn't just fall in and follow the band.

'Stand up, stand up for Jesus' isn't just a good thumping march which goes best with a brass band. It's a way of life. It's THE WAY of life – the only way, indeed, for it is Christ's way. The problems of our world, of our land, of industry, of countless thousands hearts and homes, are only there because of the simple fact that all too few folk are ready when called on, like my friend in the hospital, to speak what should be our native language – the language which God spoke when His Son our Saviour became a living word, in the flesh, here on the stage of history.

Are you always ready to speak a living word for Jesus? He'll help us to do just that if we ask Him – so we pray:

Lord, speak to me that I may speak in living accents of Thy tone.

AMEN

SAM'S BROTHER'S BAND

Somebody played a record on the radio recently of an old tune called 'In the Mood'. It started a conversation about the big dance band leaders like Joe Loss, Jack Jackson, Henry Hall and the rest. Thinking about dance bands, I remembered some years ago being on holiday in Cornwall and seeing on a few gateposts and even some trees, hand-made posters advertising a local dance and at the bottom of each poster it said, 'Music by Sam's Brother's Band.'

From that day to this it has always stuck in my mind, and each time I have recollected it I have kept wondering and wondering again who was Sam's brother – indeed who was Sam! Every one must have known Sam, I suppose, because that must have been why they named the band in such a peculiar fashion. Well, I'm no nearer the answer now than I ever was but I still feel it was a bit rough on Sam's brother not to have the band in his own name in his own right rather than to be permanently overshadowed by better known Sam. Still I suppose you might say, 'That's life'.

History books and ancient records are simply lists of famous well known names, even though we all know that none of them could have achieved what they did alone. Famous explorers, generals, mountaineers, sailors, scientists – all of these, indeed all famous folk, had others doing things that were vital, an unknown, unheralded and unsung multitude. We do well to think on this, because by far the vast majority of you, like me, belong to this multitude of ordinary folk. We are not Sam, known to all and sundry – we're only Sam's brothers and sisters. Come to think of it, there must have been a chap named Jack among my own ancestors. Everyone knew Jack, and when he had a son they called him Jackson, and again everybody knew who they were talking about, and so down the years there have been Jacksons, all following on from one well known Jack. But to go back to our dance band, it wouldn't cut any ice with the dancers that the leader of the band was Sam's brother. What they wanted and expected was a good band – never mind whose brother he was.

I claim for myself an entitlement which Jesus gave me when He said God was my Father – I claim to be God's son. But nobody is going to bother about the God part of my claim unless my part is Godlike or Christlike. I've met some folk who made such a claim, but I could never hear what they were saying because of what they were. It's no use claiming to be God's son and then being rude, or unkind, or selfish, or proud and conceited. I've heard folk make astounding claims about the Holy Spirit in their lives, and yet their family life was certainly no miniature of the Kingdom of Love – far from it.

So then, if we're only Sam's brother – let's be so good by the help of Jesus that all those with whom we come into contact will see Jesus in us and will want to belong with us to His family.

A prayer to end:

Help me in my small corner, O Lord, to be worthy of the title of being called Your son, for Your name's sake.

AMEN

A TWINKLE IN MY EYE

I have often said that one of the amazing things I have discovered through being a minister, was that over the years as I have gone into people's homes in order to minister to them – so often I have come away having been ministered unto. I went to take, and came away having received so very, very much.

Now I have an added sort of bonus blessing to my ministry, for not only does what I have just said still go on happening, but something else is happening now as well. It is this. As I go on speaking to you on Monday mornings, more and more of you write to me and so many of you are kind enough to tell me that something I have said has been a help to you. If so, Glory be to God – but here's something I want you all to know. Every week, almost every day, the letters that I get from you have ministered to me – in ways quite beyond words. Listeners' letters have been a means of grace to me and sometimes they have come with just the right word at just the right time, when I have needed them most.

I had one quite recently from a lady whose partner had gone home before her – a good man and to quote from her letter, 'full of faith and genuine goodness – who would not want me to grieve'. Isn't that great? And then she quoted a prayer for me which she said they both used. I have never seen or heard it before but, my goodness, I shall never forget it! It has meant so much to me that I simply must pass it on to you.

Lord, give me sympathy and common sense
And help me home with courage high.
Lord, give me calm and confidence,
And please – a twinkle in my eye.

Well I want the Good Lord to give me sympathy – there's much need for it. And common sense, too – I find it's far from common, it's all too rare. Calm and confidence are needed, too, in this present age of chaos and crisis – so I hope He will give me those too. But – please, please Lord – give me a twinkle in my eye! I want to say Amen and Amen to that.

How often a sense of humour has kept us going, saved a situation from complete disaster, given us the ability to keep on keeping on; and how sad it is to meet anybody who hasn't got one. But one last plea – I hope we have a twinkle in our eye when it comes to laughing at ourselves. Please, Lord, make us able to do that. I think it is so important. I think it is one of the hallmarks of the true Christian to be able from time to time to laugh at himself or herself. Yes, please, Lord, make us able to do that.

Well, here it is again, my prayer, our prayer, from my friend's letter:

Lord, give me sympathy and common sense
And help me home with courage high.
Lord, give me calm and confidence
And please – a twinkle in my eye.

AMEN

SOFTLY, SOFTLY

I became a Methodist local preacher when I was in my teens, about forty years ago, and I'm as proud to be such today as I was then – ' 'Tis worth living for this – to administer bliss and salvation in Jesus' name.'

The Methodist Circuit where it all began for me had thirty-four churches in it and sometimes a car was used to pick up a number of preachers who lived one side of the circuit and to transport them fifteen, twenty, twenty-five miles to chapels on the other side for our Sunday preaching appointments. I am eternally indebted to those older, and some very old, men for all the help and encouragement they gave to me when I began to preach. If I know anything at all about preaching today, then most of it I learned from them in those days.

I can vividly recall how one Sunday the discussion was about the unobtrusiveness of God – how in quiet, almost secret ways He goes on working His purpose out. Not with noise and brash publicity does He operate, but as quiet as a still, small voice He works sometimes on somebody's life until that person is seen to be a man, or a woman, of God.

In order to illustrate the point, this old local preacher told us a story about a once famous sculptor who also had a son who was a sculptor. With the passing of the years the father gradually lost the ability he once had, and his eyesight grew poor so that he would chisel away at the stone and produce a very poor result, but those fading eyes were unable to see his own defects. But each night, after the father had gone to bed, the son would quietly work on the stone and perfect it so that next morning when the old man began again fresh, he really thought he was still producing a masterpiece. Yes, said my old friend, the Father God takes us and He also takes our poor efforts, both so often full of blemishes, and He works on them and He quietly produces something of a beauty we alone could never hope to achieve.

With the passing of the years, that story has meant more and more to me. I've gone on in my Master's service knowing that the poorest offerings which I have made in His service He is able to take and quietly bring them to perfection. How good it is to know that we don't have to wait to serve Christ and His Kingdom until we can produce a perfect masterpiece! Instead, all we need to do is to do our very best and then to hand that to Him in the sure and certain knowledge that long after we have finished He goes on perfecting. Those efforts of ours that we would even scrap and throw on the rubbish heap, even those He takes, because He and He alone is able to make all things new. Also, in His love He is going on remaking me, and remaking you, if we will let Him.

Let's tell Him then so to do:

Dear God, create in me a clean heart and renew within me a right spirit.

AMEN

SOVEREIGN IN RESIDENCE

We have discovered something in our house. Friends who come to see us are really fascinated by this great capital city of ours, and when they are staying with us they all seem to be most anxious to do a sort of conducted sight-seeing tour. Roughly speaking, they all want to see the same things – the Houses of Parliament, Trafalgar Square, Downing Street, the Bank of England, St Paul's and the Tower of London; and always – yes always – Buckingham Palace. I always tell them when we take them to look at Buckingham Palace, 'The Queen's in'; or 'The Queen's not in today'. I tell them in a matter-of-fact sort of voice, just as though Her Majesty kept me personally daily informed of her every movement. You can get away with this sometimes, because not all our visitors know that when the Sovereign is in residence, the Royal Standard flies over the top of Buckingham Palace. It's as simple as that – the Sovereign inside and the standard shows.

I was coming past there alone quite late one evening and out of curiosity I glanced up and there it was – the standard flying – and so I knew the Sovereign was there. It set me thinking about standards. Would it be going too far for me to assert that during my lifetime I have lived to see a decline in the standards of an increasing majority of folk in this land of ours? An exaggeration? I wish it were – I'm afraid it's all too true. It may well be the 'in' thing now-a-days to scoff at the Ten Commandments, but I know in my heart of hearts that if everybody kept them this world would be a far, far better place to live in than it is now. If you will have a look at this morning's or any morning's paper and take out all the so-called news that's in it, that would not be there if folk had kept the Ten Commandments you would find that, advertisements apart, you were not left with a very big newspaper. So much of the sad and the bad and the mad reading is only there because folk have decided that standards don't matter any more and everyone just pleases himself.

I could go on now, of course, and point out that you can scrap the Ten Commandments if you are prepared fully to replace them by the Two New Commandments of Jesus – to love God utterly and to love others as much as you love yourself – but that takes a bit of doing for any man. Which brings me right back again to where I started – to Buckingham Palace. The standard is only there and flying high when the Sovereign is in residence.

I have found that the only way for a man to live up to the standards of Jesus is for him to have Jesus in residence – residing as Sovereign and Lord in his heart. Show me a man fully and utterly committed to Jesus, and I've known plenty such, and that man is the man whose standards are good and right and pure and true; and above all, his are the standards of love.

So a prayer:

Come into my heart, Lord Jesus, and rule there as Sovereign and Lord so that my life may be Christlike.

AMEN

SPARROWS, LILIES AND ME

It would be incorrect to say that one of my outstanding memories of my visit to the U.S.A. was the view from the top of the Empire State building. It is true, however, that I still remember it very clearly. You can't really understand Manhattan until you have seen it from the top, as it were. I remember, too, seeing one of the Queen liners leaving its New York pier and wishing we were on it. Yet the remembrance that stamped itself on my mind was seeing the motor cars going along the streets and avenues below, all looking like those midget toy cars that my children loved to collect and play with when they were young – cars like matchboxes on wheels. Big things seem so little and insignificant when seen from a great height.

For many years the highest hills I'd seen were those in Derbyshire and Snowdonia, but there did come a day when I saw the Jungfrau. My memories here are quite the opposite of those I recall from the high building in New York. I recall the grandeur, the vastness, the bigness of those mountain peaks – high soaring, lofty, and lost in the cloudy sky quite often.

I'm sure you must have spoken as I often have about your life and experiences. Sometimes we speak of living on the mountain tops – up above and away from all fret and fear. Life is serene and we feel secure, in command – and all about us seems little and harmless and quite insignificant. We seem to be living nearer the light and the warmth – in the sunshine, as it were – and our hearts are glad, we smile and know something of an inward calm and peace. But there are other days that most of us have experienced, too. Days when we have felt justified in describing ourselves as being down – down in the valley. We've passed through the days of shadow and suffering, and the blue sky and the sunshine have seemed to be far, far away.

It could well be that life for you seems to be in the valley.

In this vale of tears and woe, maybe you are passing through what someone once described as a glen of gloom. Let me ask you to look up – look up from the valley, because if and when you do you will see bigger things up above. You'll catch a glimpse of heights and horizons far away. These are the tomorrows that are awaiting you – these are the better days in store. Yet – and this could be true – if there should be only the valley, still look up and see, not something but Someone big enough to see you through. A God of love who made the hills and the valleys, and what is more important, who made you to be like Himself. And remember that this great Creator, this powerful God, loves you, and indeed in His only Son, Jesus, He gave Himself for you. He cares about sparrows – that's fine. He cares about lilies and sheep – that's fine. Yes, but it's even finer if you're down in the valley to recall that He cares about you. And because you need Him most down there, He is willing and waiting and wanting to be nearest at hand.

My prayer to end says:

Though I walk – and it takes a long time – through the valley of the shadow, the glen of gloom, help me always to remember that Thou art with me.

AMEN

LABELS

Among my modest hopes for my retirement is one that I have cherished for years. It has never been possible, what with moving from house to house, but over these past thirty years or so I've kept promising myself that when I moved into my last house – no more moving – then I would if possible have a little greenhouse. Well, here's hoping – but I did buy recently a little packet of plant labels. I have them ready so that at least I shall know what seeds I put in, even if they never come up. Yes, its easy to label seeds put into the boxes for the greenhouse. It's not nearly so easy to label people, and yet quite often in the Bible a person was mentioned and then a label was put on them there and then.

There was one man who was named, but it didn't stop at that, it went on to say he was an Israelite – but even that wasn't enough. Another label was added and it said 'in whom there is no guile'. What a grand world this would be if all of us were given a name and then men were told of our nationality and then a label could be attached to us that said we were 'free from guile'. What a pity there is so much duplicity in the world today! Folk ready to stoop to anything in order to gain for themselves. Not everybody's word can be trusted, and day by day new stories of double dealing arise. There seems to be less and less need for the label on which is written 'no guile' today.

I have a very dear friend who is the head of a large industrial company. I once made the silly mistake of asking him about those who worked for him, and he soon corrected me and said, 'Nobody works for me, they all work with me.' In the light of that I recall another label in the Bible – it speaks about a workman who need not be ashamed. Yes, I like that too, and even more I would like to think it was a label we could truthfully attach to far more folk than we can today, from top to bottom or the other way round if you prefer it. A new nation could come into being if all of us were workmen and women who need not be ashamed.

Another man is labelled a fox and yet another a fool, and there is also the label, 'a perfect man'. The whole range of characters is there, all deserving some label or another.

Just suppose you and I were being lined up to be labelled – what on earth would they write on yours and mine? Perhaps it doesn't matter what 'they' would write – whoever 'they might be. But Woodbine Willie in one of his moving poems talks about the time when 'we stand and look in His face' – the face of Jesus. It's the label He puts on us that matters. All I hope is that by His love and grace, when that day comes for me, He will just label me with one word – four letters – MINE.

Lord Jesus, that will be glory for me – when I am Yours and You are mine, for ever and for ever. So be it.

AMEN

Have you read the other books by John Jackson?

IT WAS ON A MONDAY MORNING

Lakeland paperback no. 287

The first book of talks from 'Prayer for the day' which John Jackson broadcast to millions of BBC radio listeners; each of his talks ends with a simple, brief prayer.

HELLO AGAIN – ANOTHER MONDAY MORNING

Lakeland paperback no. 322

Among the many showbiz people who were impressed by John Jackson's quiet sincerity Jimmy Savile OBE counts himself; in his foreword to this book he wrote: 'John Jackson's books are a knockout. If you can really grasp his quite simple message it will improve your life.'

Lakeland paperbacks are published by Marshall, Morgan and Scott – you are invited to write for a complete list of titles available from:
The Sales Manager,
Marshall, Morgan and Scott,
116 Baker Street,
London W1M 2BB

Other Lakeland paperbacks:

PRAYERS WITH A PURPOSE

Lakeland paperback no. 325

Gladys Knowlton's practical approach to prayer shares the discovery that 'prayer is a three-way business; it involves God, ourselves, and other people'. Helps readers to take appropriate action as well as putting their times of prayer into focus.

THOUGHT FOR THE WEEK – OMNIBUS EDITION

Lakeland paperback no. 302

Transcripts of C. A. Joyce's popular BBC radio broadcasts, previously published as two books. Presents quotable comments on life, inspired by the author's Bible readings and his extensive experience of human nature.

IN THE COOL OF THE DAY

Lakeland paperback no. 312

Margaret Hussey's delightful book inspired by the Benedicite; are we missing the important things in the hustle and bustle of modern life? It brings many enriching thoughts from one who can now sit back and watch it pass.

PRAYERS FROM A WOMAN'S HEART

Lakeland paperback no. 278

Judith Mattison presents the essential ingredients for a richer experience of prayer, teaching us to be real and open, in this book of sensitive free verse poems, expressing emotions common to all women.

RUN AND NOT BE WEARY

Lakeland paperback no. 320

Dwight L. Carlson, himself a medical doctor, gives a Christian answer to fatigue; he has aimed his advice to all whose lives are overscheduled or misdirected, particularly to Christian workers.